Actions Speak Louder Than Words

Actions Speak Louder Than Words

Working for non-selfishness

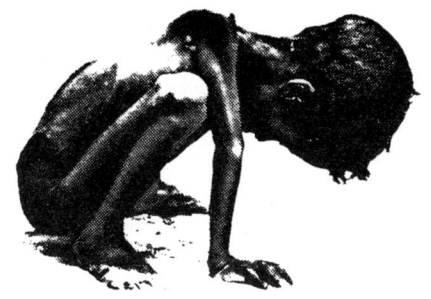

Iain Scott

HPT Books

First published in 1996
by HPT Books

HPT Books is part of
The Human Potential Trust
The Oasis, Highbrook Lane
West Hoathly
Sussex RH19 4PL, England

© 1996 by Iain Scott

No part of this book may be reproduced in any form
without the prior permission in writing of the publisher.
Brief extracts may be used by newspapers and magazines
in connection with a review.

A CIP catalogue record for this book is available
from the British Library.

Proceeds from the sale of this book, including
the author's royalties, will be used for charitable work.

ISBN 1-899131-02-7

Typeset by Jenny England, Woking, Surrey
Printed and bound by Biddles Ltd, Guildford, Surrey
Cover photograph: Awad el Sid, Sudan, at sunset.

Contents

Introduction	9
Section One: Breakthrough	13
1. Enlightenment	13
2. An historical perspective	15
3. Failure	19
4. A different approach	24
Section Two: Unnecessary suffering - the need for change	29
5. Self-orientated behaviour	29
6. Indicators of suffering	33
i. War	33
ii. Crime	37
iii. Substance abuse	38
iv. Other addictions	41
v. The pain of broken intimacy and isolation	43
vi. Non-human suffering	44
7. Tears are not enough.....	48
8. A waste of money.....a waste of life	54
Section Three: Why is it so difficult to change?	61
9. Conditioning	61
10. Avoidance	66
11. Forgetfulness	70
12. Excuses	72
13. Complacency	75

14. The "I want more" mentality	78
15. Half-full or half-empty?	81
16. The burden of responsibility	84
17. Emotional imbalance	88
18. Self-expression	92
19. Get over it!	96
20. The fear of letting go	100
21. Awareness is not the same as achievement	103
22. The blind leading the blind	106
23. Heading for chaos?	109
24. An "impossible dream"?	112
Section Four: Non-selfishness	115
25. Approaching the start-line	115
26. The formula for change	122
27. The anti-hypocrisy test	131
28. The next step forward in human evolution	136
Epilogue: And on.....and on...?	143

This book is dedicated to the memory of
the 15-year-old Ethiopian girl who died in my arms in 1985.
Weakened by famine and ravaged by illness, a few pence
worth of medicine could have almost
certainly saved her life.

She may be gone - but she is not forgotten.

Acknowledgements

Thank you to everyone who read and commented on the draft manuscript. I am also grateful to Dieter Saur for checking a fact in Germany after we met one evening in Nepal.

Permission to quote lyrics from several songs was kindly granted with assistance by Phillip Keith of IMP on behalf of Warner Chappell Music, and by Diane Hayes of Rondor Music for the following:

> *We Are The World* by USA for Africa
> *Do They Know It's Christmas?* by Band Aid
> *Tears Are Not Enough* by Northern Lights
> *Never Is Too Late* by Joan Armatrading
> *The Last Resort* by The Eagles.

Sarah, my wife and colleague, has been fully involved throughout. Her contributions have been many and varied. I am sure that Sarah's own personal example, as outlined in the Introduction, will be of help and inspiration to others.

Introduction

I was raped at the age of 10. Tricked by a stranger, he threatened to kill me if I wasn't quiet, before violating me. My nice safe childhood world was shattered.

A few days later as the shock began to lessen, still terrified by what had happened, I plucked up enough courage to tell my parents late one evening. They listened to me and seemed to understand before settling me back in bed. But that was all. Nothing more was ever said. My parents took the easy course, hoping that the abuse would be forgotten. The police were not told that I had been raped, leaving the rapist free, presumably to rape again. I was not medically examined nor counselled.

I was left to cope with the trauma on my own. Over the next couple of years, I was anxious that I could be pregnant or might have some sexually-transmitted disease. Part of me withdrew into my own inner world. As I grew up, this was increasingly interrupted by reminders whenever rape was mentioned on television or discussed by friends. I felt embarrassed and awkward at these times.

At the age of 20, I turned to my sister for help. When I told her what had happened to me, she was more preoccupied with her own feelings than mine. I was still alone.

I eventually met Iain – now my husband – and found the understanding, care, and support necessary to help me. I have gradually faced, worked through, and overcome the past years of trauma. Extreme avoidance, over-sensitivity, withdrawal, self-hatred, misplaced guilt, isolation, self-pity, and a lack of self-worth have now been constructively replaced with a healthy non-selfish attitude to life. I know from personal experience what it is like to suffer as a result of selfishness. Putting what you want before the needs of others does not work. The self-orientated mind-set that people accept as normal causes untold suffering. Rape is just one of the more obvious examples of this insensitive strategy. My life is now dedicated to taking less and giving more. We have got to learn a better way of living together.

Sarah Scott

Why does someone rape an innocent child? What kind of society produces such extreme psychological sickness? To what degree are we all responsible? And how can these atrocities be prevented? These are questions that must be answered. This is a real issue which cannot be ignored.

The rape of a 10-year-old child is an extreme reminder of how people use and abuse each other. Such horrific crimes make blatantly clear that we must develop beyond the twisted justifications and small-mindedness of self-interest. Thousands of years of religion and philosophy have so far failed to end the suffering. Laws prohibiting offences such as rape, backed up by the police and other law enforcement agencies, have likewise been unable to stop these outrages. We need a solution. We have to find a new way of behaving towards each other – a more mature way of interacting with the world around us. Any potential solution to the many widespread problems must be practical. The rhetoric of intelligent-sounding words is not enough. There can be no room for hypocrisy.

This is a book that will challenge you. It might make you feel uncomfortable, pointing out things which some would rather avoid. It is not a book about rape, nor one just dealing with the equally sickening obscenities of third world poverty. Rather, it is a plea for human beings to take what may prove to be the next step forward in our evolution. It is a book about standing back, questioning

Introduction

limitations and presumptions, then starting again with a fresh perspective. It is about facing reality. The contents are essential and relevant to us all – presented in a straightforward, no-hype, no-frills, and no-nonsense manner. Hopefully, it is a book that will make you think more, care more, and do more.....

Iain Scott
Sussex, February 1996

SECTION ONE: BREAKTHROUGH

1

Enlightenment

Beginning in the summer of 1975, a series of oneness experiences changed my life. I described the initial event in *Human Potential – the search for that "something more"* as follows:

> *Late one evening, I experienced an astonishing expansion of consciousness. Timeless moments of ecstasy and oneness revealed a reality I had not previously considered. There was an intense awareness of the unity of everything and everyone. Life had an obvious meaning and purpose. This mental awareness was matched by an equally intense feeling of love, caring, and belonging. I could see the problems facing our world and also a solution to them.*
>
> *There was an incredible sense of needing to help others – not in any compulsive or unbalanced way, but rather because service was the natural thing to do. My selfish tendencies had effortlessly melted away, although I still retained an appreciation of individuality. There was no separateness, only oneness.*

What happened was completely unexpected and apparently spontaneous. I had never heard of mystical experiences or any mention of such a dramatic change of awareness. I was not practising meditation, nor had I taken any mind-expanding drugs. I had a practical, no-nonsense upbringing and was training as a biologist. The sudden shift of consciousness was profound.

Dozens of additional oneness experiences quickly

followed during the next few weeks, each having a powerful effect on my perception, thinking, feeling, values, and actions. Later, I read a number of books about altered states of mind – but most seemed to lack first-hand knowledge and/or failed to offer a proper explanation of what was happening to me. The spontaneous process of transformation meanwhile continued, with repeated insights into this "new" non-selfish consciousness bringing increasing familiarity and greater understanding. If the first few oneness experiences had initially awakened me from the blinkered world of ordinary awareness, the frequent on-going exposure reinforced this awakening. Between these direct experiences of unity, the links to normal consciousness became progressively weakened and insignificant.

Then, in 1978, a final realisation removed the last mental barrier of any remaining ordinary consciousness. The perception and feeling of interconnectedness has since stayed with me as a constant and continual experience. This "new" consciousness is real and a beneficial alternative to that of normal self-orientated behaviour. It is usually referred to as enlightenment. I call it non-selfishness.

My actions have changed considerably as a result of the transformation, with concern for the needs of the whole replacing the dominating wants of normal or ordinary consciousness. The way I look at life now differs significantly from before. I see billions of human beings acting in a basically selfish manner. From my perspective, there is little difference in behaviour between so-called "good" and so-called "bad" people – compared to the huge potential offered by genuine non-selfishness. Society has a severely limited idea of what is "good" and "bad", involving a great deal of hypocrisy and finger-pointing. Standards which may presently be socially acceptable and conventionally desirable are a long way from being completely altruistic or non-selfish. Human beings are psychologically immature to varying degrees, still in the early stages of development. Non-selfishness offers a clear way forward from this troublesome infancy towards a more balanced way of living.

2

An historical perspective

Others before me have experienced this breakthrough in consciousness. Throughout history, at least for the past three thousand years or so, occasional individuals have known the oneness of life. Distinct parallels or similarities stand out in their various recorded testimonies, indicating that the same non-selfish potential has been repeatedly realised as the way forward.

A number of academics have come to the same conclusion after carefully studying the world's spiritual teachings, mystical writings, and great poetry. For example, Professor David Fontana – an internationally-respected psychologist and educationalist – commented on *Human Potential – the search for that "something more"* in the following way:

> *The first thing to say about the book is that it records a remarkable and clearly authentic experience. Without prior reading in the area, you nevertheless achieved states which mirror exactly those recorded by mystics in all the great spiritual traditions. The sense of the small, limited self is lost in the oceanic awareness of love and unity. It is given to very few people to have this experience of knowing as opposed to merely believing, and I am glad that you have been able to put the experience on paper for the benefit of others.*
>
> *The second thing is that the methods towards this enlightened state which you outline are very much those taught, with small variations in detail, in Buddhism, Hinduism, Sufism and the Western mystery traditions. This provides further proof of the authenticity of your experience.*

Actions Speak Louder Than Words

Enlightenment has been called various different names. Liberation, cosmic consciousness, satori, Buddhahood, the Kingdom of Heaven, samadhi, gnãna, moksha, the Tao, and self-realisation are some of the common descriptions used throughout the world. It has been traditionally symbolised by images such as the thousand-petalled lotus flower, the eternal flame, and the top of a mountain. Those who have achieved complete understanding or enlightenment have been called avatars, prophets, Buddhas, or Messiahs.

Experiencing a glimpse of oneness may be profound and even transforming to varying extents, but such instances should not be confused with genuine enlightenment. The vast majority of mystical insights are followed by a return to self-orientated consciousness, albeit with the memory or knowledge that a higher awareness is available; selfishness remains or creeps back in. Unfortunately, some have equated or mistaken their heightened insight with true enlightenment – thus the warnings about being cautious of "false prophets".

It should also be realised that there are different degrees of exposure involved in experiences of unity or interconnectedness. These glimpses might be partial or incomplete, limited by the individual's capacity or preparedness to totally let go. Therefore, a full-blown oneness experience is probably much rarer than a partial exposure to this tremendous potential – although both will be felt as powerful and awe-inspiring. Furthermore, the occurrence will usually be interpreted (at the time and/or afterwards) according to the person's religious and cultural influences, perhaps creating distortions.

These oneness experiences can appear to happen spontaneously – like in my own instance – or as a result of pursuing some intentional exercise or discipline such as meditation. Whether an individual is seeking awakening or not, a sudden exposure to the interconnectedness experience must be prompted by certain psychological triggers (and, conversely, hampered by certain psychological restrictions). It is unlikely that the cause is so-

An historical perspective

called "divine grace", as has often been presumed. However, when the aspirant has been following a demanding ascetic procedure like fasting or the frenzied whirling of dervish dancing, mystical insights could have been provoked by the resulting changes in body chemistry.

Biological triggers are more obvious when certain plants, known to have mind-altering or hallucinogenic properties, are eaten. For example, the peyote cactus and various mushrooms have long been used by a number of cultures to produce heightened feelings and visions as part of their spiritual rituals and ceremonies. In recent times, the psychedelic drug LSD has been widely taken as the modern equivalent. Although not always used for the purpose of seriously exploring the hidden areas of the mind, numerous people have nevertheless reported varying glimpses of the mystical experience during such drug-induced "trips". Generally, these mind-altering plants and illegal drugs seem to act as nothing more than unspecific amplifiers and de-inhibitors. (Please note that in mentioning the historical fact of people taking naturally occurring plants and synthetically produced drugs with psychedelic properties, I am neither implying that they are helpful in any real way nor suggesting their use.)

This "new" expanded consciousness has also been glimpsed by some of the astronauts. It seems to have been triggered by the breathtaking sight of planet Earth floating in the vastness of space. Seeing the marvellous spectacle of our planet as a beautiful blue and white jewel suspended against the blackness of space is clearly capable of producing a shift of perspective. The feeling of being privileged to experience such a distant view of "home" seems to have interacted with the realisation that billions of fellow human beings were meanwhile continuing their various exploitative "I want" daily activities. This combined realisation then appears to have evoked an awareness of the need for a radical solution to overcome all the global problems and personal pettiness. Edgar D. Mitchell – the sixth man to walk on the moon – coined the term "instant global consciousness" to describe this heightened awareness experienced by himself and other fellow astronauts.

To summarise this brief overview, a tiny minority of people throughout history – from different parts of the world – have experienced a glimpse of interconnectedness to varying degrees. Such personal testimonies repeatedly point to an authentic potential breakthrough in the evolution of consciousness, going beyond the limitations of self-ishness. However, these powerful temporary exposures should not be confused with true enlightenment. A few individuals would appear to have achieved this breakthrough as a constant experience or realisation, dissolving all self-orientated tendencies. This completeness of understanding, on-going identification with the whole, and non-selfish service to others is the future potential for humankind.

Placing my own case in the context of this overview, (as briefly described in Chapter 1), I had dozens of full-blown exposures to the oneness of life beginning in 1975. These culminated with a final "coming together" or complete enlightenment in 1978, which has since remained as a constant experience. I am making this clear so that it can be understood from what perspective these words are written.

3

Failure

I did not and still do not see the need to interpret these tremendous insights of unity and interconnectedness as a matter of religious belief. It is unnecessary to do so. I prefer to focus attention on the basic issue of non-selfishness – which is a straightforward matter of behaviour, non-dependent upon any particular belief. Non-selfishness can stand on its own merits, whatever the nature of people's beliefs.

As a biologist, I consider that the development of this "new" non-selfish consciousness is the next step forward in human evolution. It is a potential which has so far only been experienced by a relatively few individuals – whereas it needs to be known to and developed by every individual, when it would then radically transform the human race and its effects on our planet. For this to happen, exact knowledge and a process of education will be required – equally matched by appropriate action – rather than the traditional dependency upon belief.

If we are honest, religion and philosophy have so far failed to fundamentally change human behaviour. Millions may believe or be interested in some better way, which to some limited degree might influence their actions, but they nevertheless remain in the same self-orientated consciousness. Widespread inhumanity continues on a daily basis. Suffering goes on and on. Any effort towards transformation to date has simply not been good enough.

Siddhartha Gautama, the Buddha, lived approximately 2500 years ago and Jesus lived approximately 2000 years ago – to name just two pioneers of this "new" consciousness. Many generations have since had the life-long opportunity to learn from their wise teachings. Yet the vast majority of Buddhists and Christians seem content to merely believe and modify their behaviour. There is generally a distinct lack of serious, mature intention to gain the same heightened consciousness.....and an even greater absence of individuals who have actually succeeded. The followers seem stuck on following, rather than willing and able to completely achieve the potential of non-selfishness.

Two examples should help illustrate the point that Buddhism and Christianity have so far failed to deliver any fundamental shift of behaviour. (My intention is to constructively examine the effect of these world religions, as opposed to negatively condemn them.) Part of the Buddha's teachings specifies the need for compassion towards living creatures, indicating a vegetarian diet. And yet numerous Buddhists, including many monks and nuns, choose to eat meat. They conveniently side-step the forbidden act of slaughtering the animals themselves by letting others do the actual killing – ignoring the market reality that it is done on their behalf. In Bhutan, local oxen are driven to the top of a steep cliff by herders and then pushed off.....so that the monks can justify their actions by saying that the meat comes from animals which have died a "natural" death!

The second example focuses on one of Jesus' central teachings as expressed by his words: "Do to others as you would have them do to you." The instruction is simple and straightforward: behave towards others as you would like to be treated by them if the situation was reversed. So why do most Christians spend more money on a new car, a holiday, cosmetics, fashionable clothes, or whatever – i.e. things for themselves – than they give to help those in third world countries who continue to suffer and die because of absolute poverty? And would their defensive response to searching questions like this be the same if the roles *were* reversed and they lived as poor villagers somewhere like Ethiopia or Sudan?

The majority of those interested in a better non-selfish way are clearly having difficulties in realising it as a practical reality. Either their conceptual understanding of the nature of the change and/or their knowledge of how to do it is limited, or else their application of the principles falls short in practice through inadequate motivation – or both. Perhaps the few of us who have experienced this complete breakthrough in consciousness have failed to adequately explain the "how to" process – or died before it had got a firm foundation, after which time the teachings are then partly misunderstood and distorted by those still in a limited state of mind. Some of the early pioneers who experienced this potential may not even have precisely understood the phenomenon. In my own case, logic and scientific methodology – learned during my training in biology, which I was already undertaking when the oneness experiences began – may have helped me clearly sort out what is involved in this dramatic process of transformation. Furthermore, prior to the final enlightenment, I was catapulted into a state of knowing interconnectedness on dozens of occasions – returning to normal consciousness in between these powerful and purging glimpses – and so was able to repeatedly observe the differences of these two alternatives.

I was well aware of this fact of failure when I spoke openly during 1978/1979 after my enlightenment. It was blatantly obvious that everyone I met was trapped by normal consciousness – constantly reinforced through ongoing conditioning, generation after generation. Even those individuals who were knowingly searching for that "something more", some perhaps well-read in the various spiritual traditions, were entangled and hindered. So it didn't take much extra reasoning to work out that the pioneers before me had failed in their objective of stimulating a widespread radical breakthrough in consciousness. Going a step further forward in this thinking raised the possibility that I might also fail.....

As interest in what had happened to me grew, I was therefore alert to the prospect of possible failure. There was a danger of me repeating the same efforts as the former pioneers of non-selfishness, which had obviously been lacking in some way. After a number of months, it became clear to me that the people whom I was trying to help were not properly changing or developing. On the face of it, most of them seemed to be gradually changing – and in their opinion of themselves, some assured me that they definitely were. But from my perspective, any progress was at best limited and at worst self-deceptive. Almost everyone who had regularly met with me over the months, asking questions about this expanded potential, was developing in an unbalanced way. They were thinking more and feeling more, but their outer actions remained largely unaltered.

It seemed that this internal growth was little more than just another expression of self-interest – despite the fact that the individuals involved were well-meaning and serious by normal standards, many having had a long interest in spirituality and the development of consciousness. Their behaviour remained basically self-orientated. They may have understood more and felt more at times, but the effect of this only trickled out towards others in comparatively small ways. It was not the same as the beginning of a genuine shift towards non-selfishness.

When I examined what was happening, it became increasingly clear that the same pattern was being repeated by everyone. I had no difficulty in stimulating different thoughts and increased feeling in others – but, left to their own freedom of choice, this internalisation failed to translate into appropriate outer actions of an equivalent degree. The grip of people's self-orientated mind-set was challenged, but not significantly weakened. Every individual seemed fooled by their internal development as if this apparent change was somehow enough. But increased awareness was not enough. They failed to sufficiently realise that any expansion of understanding and caring must be matched with a corresponding degree of non-selfish outer action. Or perhaps they lacked the necessary motivation or integrity to overcome their own hypocrisy. Whatever, their thoughts and feelings were apparently moving towards non-selfishness – but they still demonstrated self-orientated behaviour in the actions of everyday life.

Failure

I could see that further effort along the same lines would merely deepen this false impression of development. I wondered if other enlightened pioneers before me had failed to properly discern or work out that such a difficulty existed? Or perhaps they just hoped that this imbalance would somehow gradually sort itself out? So, knowing the history of failure and alert to the risk that my efforts could likewise fail, I decided to stop talking about this "new" consciousness. After a final two-week period of answering people's questions following an announcement of my decision, I moved away to re-think what might be the key to a successful approach.

4

A different approach

I was sure that my understanding of the formula necessary for change was correct. It was logical, all-embracing, and always checked-out practically when matched against real-life situations. A number of serious-minded people had listened on repeated occasions, attempting to learn, gradually seeming to understand – yet their actions remained largely self-orientated and therefore effectively unchanged. It was probable that those interested were filtering what I was saying, wanting to develop but nevertheless still only hearing what they wanted to hear. Although I had pointed out the tendency that most people do not want to know what the problem with them is, this warning and other cautionary remarks were likely not enough. Somehow, the approach taken by myself and those pioneers before me was inadequate.....leading to failure and a continuation of normal consciousness. What would it take to stimulate a genuine and sustainable breakthrough in others?

The same weakness of response had showed up in everyone – i.e. a distinct lack of appropriate non-selfish action, despite an increase in thinking and caring. This deficiency identified the area in need of extra emphasis. Developing non-selfish giving and service would have to be more explicitly incorporated into the educational process, making totally clear that this was a crucially important requisite for change. If participants willing to shift consciousness could not work out for themselves what should have been obvious – perhaps due to their conditioned avoidance and the tight grip of self-preoccupation – then the need for non-selfish action on a step-by-step basis would have to be bluntly pointed out. Although such an approach might at first appear confrontational to someone with a defensive state of mind – and self-

A different approach

protection is typical of normal consciousness – the strategy of adopting increased bluntness had to be a gamble worth taking in order to overcome the impasse.

To provide practical demonstration projects of non-selfish giving and service, I spent a number of years establishing two charities: You And Me and The Wildlife For All Trust. Third world poverty and nature conservation are two areas of need most urgently requiring attention. Both sets of problems occur as a consequence of selfishness and any real solution will have to involve a greater concern for the whole. I reasoned that the opportunity for genuine altruistic involvement with this practical work, combined with clear education about how to make the shift towards non-selfishness, would create the means for a potential breakthrough of consciousness in others to be achieved.

All charities have the aim of assisting certain beneficiaries in need of help. However, it is pertinent to point out that such organisations are operated from a perspective of normal or ordinary consciousness, albeit with a well-meaning charitable motivation. You And Me and The Wildlife For All Trust, in contrast, have been and continue to be run from an alternative perspective. I have guarded our charities against many of the self-orientated considerations or pitfalls which limit the efficiency and effectiveness of most organisations. We therefore differ considerably in some respects from other charities with regards to our way of working; non-selfish awareness significantly enhances the spirit of charitable service and giving.

My original plan was to first establish the wildlife work, then begin to talk openly again about what had happened to me and the non-selfish alternative, and thirdly to establish another charity with the aim of helping to relieve third world poverty and suffering. A 9-acre site in the Sussex countryside was accordingly purchased and gradually developed into the beginnings of a nature reserve and outdoor educational centre. Officially designated as part of an Area of Outstanding Natural Beauty, the site was named The Oasis. Our preliminary investigations revealed that a number of Australian wallabies were endangered or vulnerable, yet "forgotten" by the international conservation movement. We therefore started The Wallaby Concern, (now part of The Wildlife For All Trust).

As outlined in the first part of *Human Potential – the search for that "something more"*, the Ethiopian famine of 1984/1985 altered the above-mentioned plans. The wildlife work was effectively suspended so that our efforts could be mainly directed towards carrying out relief and development work, moving from Ethiopia to Sudan as the emergency lessened. We thus established the You And Me charity earlier than intended. Awad el Sid in Sudan became the focus of our practical demonstration project – helping several thousand Ethiopian and Eritrean refugees, as well as tens of thousands of poor Sudanese villagers. We have purposely worked non-paid, not least in response to the inefficiency and ineffectiveness of most other charities. A medical health clinic has formed the heart of our activities, which has now been successfully running for over ten years at the time of writing. The clinic offers free treatment for a wide range of general and tropical illnesses, together with health education as a preventative measure. You And Me quickly gained a reputation amongst the Sudanese people and Ethiopian/ Eritrean refugees as an organisation which genuinely puts the humanitarian considerations first beyond all other factors. Whilst most other aid agencies spend money on new 4WD vehicles but often run out of medical supplies, for example, I have personally made sure that our clinic is always well-stocked with the necessary range of essential medical drugs and equipment. My wife and colleague, Sarah, together with Mrs Sundous Mohammed Abdel Aziz, our Sudanese director, have both greatly helped maintain the high standards of excellence which I aimed to demonstrate through this project. Over 35,000 patients are currently being examined, diagnosed, and treated each year.

As the You And Me work became well-established, we were once again able to concentrate on the issue of nature conservation and so The Wildlife For All Trust was formally registered. Specialising in "forgotten" or largely-neglected

A different approach

areas, our main projects involve helping to save a number of endangered and vulnerable Australian wallabies from the threat of extinction, together with the endangered Geometric Tortoise and its threatened renosterveld habitat in the Western Cape of South Africa. More generally, it is clear to us that the environmental movement as it is today will probably only achieve a limited amount of success at best. The balance of nature has been upset by human greed and we think that the problem is unlikely to be truly solved so long as people remain stuck in the "I want more" mentality. This fundamental cause of environmental decline must be properly understood by everyone and a major change of lifestyle promoted as a basic part of the solution. The conservation ethic needs to be deepened in both approach and application.

I had planned to begin talking openly again about non-selfishness during 1985. But these plans were postponed in case it caused some confusion and misunderstanding about the nature of my intentions with regards to the emergency relief work. People were dying in Ethiopia and Sudan, with many more unnecessarily suffering, and I thought it best to maintain a simple humanitarian profile. Donors from all walks of life were trusting me to act on their behalf – and the need for assistance in Africa was urgent. I decided that a few more years of keeping quiet hopefully would not be wasted time in the long-run.

By the beginning of 1994, with almost a decade of the You And Me work successfully achieved and Wildlife For All's projects now well under way, the timing seemed right to resume speaking out about my enlightenment and the all-important issue of non-selfishness. I immediately wrote *Human Potential – the search for that "something more"* during February/March as a basic, simple-to-read reference book. The first section provides an introductory explanation – outlining the oneness experiences and subsequent transformation, together with a brief account of my activities between 1978 and 1994. The second section details the way forward – a "how to" guide for others willing to make the shift of consciousness. I purposely tried to keep the contents as simple and straightforward as possible. Some sentences require a lot of consideration and extensive personal reflection for the book's real usefulness to become clear. I was well aware that the majority of readers would read it once or perhaps twice, probably agreeing with most or all of the words, yet fail to take advantage of its intended use as a guidebook outlining a precise formula for change. Too many people are caught up in the compulsive act of searching, rarely stopping to properly study and learn. Uncomfortable choices are generally avoided. Furthermore, they usually become distracted by entertaining mumbo-jumbo, unnecessary philosophy, and superficial experiences.

To facilitate the work of promoting non-selfishness, we next set up the third of our "sister" charities. The Human Potential Trust is registered as an educational organisation. Its objectives are to carry out educational activities designed to bring about non-selfishness and also to encourage appropriate research into the subject where necessary. This book, for example, is part of our informative endeavours.

The Human Potential Trust, You And Me, and The Wildlife For All Trust therefore together form an integrated approach. Hopefully, this extra emphasis on the need to demonstrate practical non-selfish giving and service will help make clear our essential anti-hypocrisy test: actions speak louder than words.

SECTION TWO:
UNNECESSARY SUFFERING – THE NEED FOR CHANGE

5
Self-orientated behaviour

Normal or ordinary consciousness is characterised by self-orientated behaviour. It is based on self-ish desire: the "I want" or "I want more" mentality. You are primarily concerned about what you want for yourself – or maybe for yourself and your family – instead of being concerned for the needs of everyone and everything. This self-preoccupation leaves little time to think about others in a truly balanced way. It is more to do with being thought-less and care-less, instead of being completely thought-full and care-full. Normal consciousness is therefore a prejudiced state of mind, heavily biased towards self-ish considerations and so less concerned about the whole of life. To be bluntly honest, it could be generally described as a life of "me, me, me" or "take, take, take".

The self-orientated mind-set is a limited condition. Even when individuals have learned to use their potential abilities and are able to express themselves – harnessing to an exceptional degree their freedom of choice – there are still limitations. "Good" people committed to charity work, for example, are likewise restricted. These restrictions are a predictable consequence of the self-orientated strategy. When self-ish desire comes first, you have to somehow cut-off from the needs of others to a greater or lesser degree.

You avoid what is difficult and/or inconvenient, perhaps taking the course of least resistance. You see what you want to see. You do what you want to do. At times, it is easier to ignore or forget than to face harsh reality. This avoidance determines the limitations.

As everyone's experience is a unique combination of outer events and inner responses, each individual has developed a unique strategy for living. Some are more successful at getting what they want than others. Some appear more aware and caring than others. Some have ambitious goals, whilst others seem content just to get by with the minimum of bother. Some conduct their lives according to a distinct moral code of conscience or belief, whereas others try to get what they want in a more aggressive and blatantly selfish way. In short, some are at the healthier end of the self-orientated spectrum and others are at the less healthy end – with the majority of people somewhere between these two extremes. From my perspective, however, almost all human beings are currently functioning within this range of self-orientated behaviour.

The nature of normal consciousness is inherently problematic. The "I want" or "I want more" desire results in an endless cycle of "ups" and "downs". There is a mixture of satisfaction and dissatisfaction. As this desire is self-orientated to a greater or lesser extent, there are going to be "winners" and "losers". And suffering. Whilst there is selfishness, there cannot be genuine and constant unity. This is true both on a personal and global level. Ordinary consciousness is dysfunctional, even though there are degrees of happiness and success as well as suffering and failure within this overall situation.

Many people are interested in personal growth, the development of consciousness, spirituality, or whatever you want to call it, but the vast majority of these individuals underestimate the scale of change involved. They frequently fail to stand back enough, so as to appreciate that two completely different alternatives are available – never really

Self-orientated behaviour

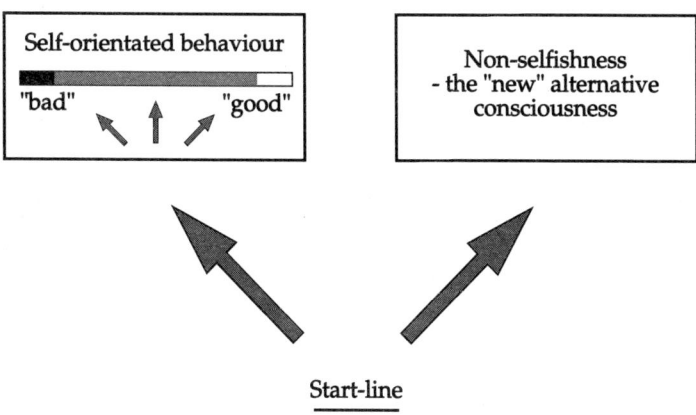

getting to the start-line for beginning a real shift of consciousness. With only very rare exceptions, their well-meaning efforts invariably amount to little more than moving to the healthier end of the range of self-orientated behaviour.....if that. There has been a widespread failure in realising the extent of self-ishness. People usually mistake less selfish behaviour for non-selfishness. They misunderstand this "new" alternative consciousness and do not fully realise what is required to make the shift. Therefore, there is no real choice created – no reasonable chance of succeeding. People thus remain stuck within the limited parameters of the self-orientated mind-set. There is no true awakening, only perpetual denial. What seems like increased awareness still fails to illuminate the whole picture or the fundamental problem. An analogy used in *Human Potential – the search for that "something more"* is relevant to help stress this fact:

> *The teacher remarked to the pupil: "Your problem is that you are seeing double." "Impossible!" replied the pupil. "If that were so, there would be four suns in the sky instead of two!"*

A lifetime of conditioning has made ordinary consciousness seem acceptable and normal to you. It is what you know. It is what others around you know. Avoidance and denial have helped maintain the self-orientated agenda. For those who have considered the non-selfish alternative, it is perceived as a hazy ideal, a belief, a theoretical possibility, a distant goal, and/or a mystery. Even for the tiny minority who have to some degree briefly glimpsed this potential, such an experience will have been of little help in achieving constant non-selfishness. Learning how to burst your own bubble – to penetrate the grip of selfishness – is not an easy thing to do. The task may be known to you as a possible goal or destination, but the route to accomplishment remains vague. Numerous individuals have seriously attempted to gain enlightenment throughout the many years and generations gone by.....and failed. Few have genuinely known this alternative as an on-going reality. To stand any chance of success, you need precise education – a guide and clear reference points – based on genuine knowledge developed through direct experience. Otherwise, it is probable that your attempts at change will result in a fumbled shift merely within the range of normal consciousness. Do not confuse activity with achievement, nor becoming a healthier or "good" person with the radical alternative of non-selfishness.

6

Indicators of suffering

The common consequence of self-orientated behaviour is suffering. This suffering occurs either as a result of a person's own selfish desires or due to another's selfish actions. As normal consciousness is essentially dysfunctional, some kind of breakdown is sooner or later going to occur. Happiness is unlikely to remain constant for very long, unless the level of contentment is limited to minimise the risk of potential disappointment. Selfishness inevitably leads to dilemma and conflict at some level – individual, family, community, or world – with suffering a calamity waiting to happen.

The majority of all personal and global suffering occurs because of the selfish nature of normal consciousness. This suffering is unnecessary. It would not occur in a world where non-selfishness had replaced the current self-orientated behaviour. Personal suffering and the distress of others provides a compelling reason or motivation for change. Suffering is a consequence of the culture of selfishness. The following indicators are intended to demonstrate the widespread nature of suffering and to show that the self-orientated mind-set is responsible in each case.

i. War

People have been making war against their fellow human beings throughout history. For example, peace was supposedly established in 1945 at the end of World War II; since then, during the so-called "post war" era, there have been approximately 160 armed conflicts. There are the major wars between nations, involving whole countries fighting against other countries. However, armed disputes between different sovereign states are more frequently isolated to cross-border skirmishes, rather than full-scale warfare. Then there are the internal conflicts, ranging from outright civil war to regional uprisings involving rebellious factions who perhaps employ protracted guerilla tactics. Finally, terrorists are usually small groups of people attempting to wage a limited type of war, using terror as a means of pressure, against the government of their own country or against that of another. In all forms of armed conflict, people get injured and killed. Many ex-soldiers have reflected during their old age that wars result in no winners – only the dead, the crippled, and the bereaved. War is destructive.

Wars have been caused by greed, the lust for power, intolerance, and fear. They may begin after a period of heightened political tension and an initial war of words. One side starts the physical aggression, then the other side responds to resist it. Innocent people get sucked into a bloody conflict which they never wanted. Individuals who might otherwise have been of basically peaceful intentions find themselves in a situation of kill or be killed. When faced with an aggressor who is hell-bent on conquering, the issue of freedom becomes an important consideration – often taken for granted if never before threatened – which might be judged worth fighting for to preserve. And so the flood gates open. The chaos and carnage begins.

The barbarity of normal consciousness can be quickly exposed during a war situation. Conventional restrictions usually applied to living in a more-or-less stable society might cease to be binding, no longer worth following. When one individual gains dominance over another from the opposing side, perhaps fuelled by hatred for "the enemy", brutal and callous behaviour becomes likely. Once uninhibited, the savageness of selfishness may run riot.

The following incident illustrates the above point. A British officer was captured in the summer of 1942 by the invading Japanese army during World War II and imprisoned in Changi, Singapore. He and other Allied prisoners of war were periodically taken from their jail to

Indicators of suffering

clean up the city streets. One day, a heavily pregnant woman passed by and was stopped by two of the Japanese soldiers guarding the working party. After briefly talking to this local woman whose country they were occupying, the two Japanese guards ripped off her dress. The British officer and his fellow POWs moved forward to help her, but were restrained by the other Japanese soldiers. One of the two guards then pulled out his bayonet and split open the woman's stomach. A Japanese officer came along and, after reprimanding the soldiers, explained to the Allied POWs that the two guards had been betting on the sex of the woman's unborn child. This mindless act of barbarity focused the attention of the British officer and his colleagues as to the kind of people who were now in charge of them. They – and thousands of other Allied POWs – subsequently experienced countless instances of needless cruelty by the Japanese before the war finally ended in 1945. Over 300,000 people died whilst prisoners of the Japanese, despite the international Geneva Convention urging the humane treatment of all POWs. Imprisoned civilian women and girls were repeatedly raped by both Japanese officers and soldiers alike – the so-called "comfort women" whose harrowing story is finally emerging after 50 years of suppression and denial.

The Holocaust also happened during World War II. 6 million Jews died in what became known as the worst case of genocide in history. Underlying racial tensions escalated into a policy of naked anti-Semitism. In 1941, the "final solution" began. At first, thousands of Jews were shot or hanged by Nazi death squads. But it soon became clear to the Nazi leaders that other methods of killing were required for dealing with the huge numbers of Jewish people involved. Death camps and gas chambers were thus constructed to provide a more efficient and impersonal means of annihilation. Millions of Jews were transported to extermination camps in remote parts of Poland. These places, such as Auschwitz and Treblinka, became industrial killing centres. Their purpose was the speedy and efficient production of mass death, including the processing of the by-products. Jews were usually "processed" within hours of their arrival. Most of the main extermination camps operated from 1941 to the end of 1944.

Each train delivered between 1000 and 3000 Jews, crammed into sealed compartments. On arrival, a few were selected for work. Most were stripped and shaved, then packed into the gas chambers. Afterwards, Jewish labour squads were ordered to extract gold teeth and fillings before removing the bodies for cremation. To then destroy the evidence, the ashes were used as fertiliser on SS farms or else dumped in nearby marshes. All possessions, clothes, and hair of the victims was sorted, marked, and sent back to Germany for re-use. The hair, for example, was utilised for the insulation of submarines and for making fabric, socks, and mattresses. The fat which dripped from the burned bodies was often collected in ditches dug for that purpose near the incineration sites, then used for fuelling subsequent cremations. Human skin was sometimes made into lampshades. During the summer of 1944, over half a million Hungarian Jews were gassed in less than two months at the Auschwitz killing centre.

It would be mistaken to think that what happened during World War II was an isolated event. Genocide has occurred since. In 1972, over 100,000 Hutus were massacred by the ruling Tutsi tribe in the small African country of Burundi. Up to 3 million Bengalis were massacred by the Pakistan army during the same year. The Khmer Rouge murdered 2 million Cambodians in Kampuchea during the late 1970s. Again in Africa, half a million Rwandans were brutally killed in April 1994, mainly Hutus against the Tutsi tribal minority; this human tragedy then continued as huge numbers of Rwandans fled to form refugee camps at places like Goma on the border of Zaire. In Europe, the fighting in former Yugoslavia (1991–1995) between people who were once neighbours has been characterised by many examples of "ethnic cleansing", including the use of systematic rape.

ii. Crime

Criminal activity has been a growing worldwide trend in recent decades. Individual countries usually record millions of crimes each year. Estimates indicate that the real figures are several times greater than those officially registered. It is no longer safe to leave your door unlocked. Even with modern security devices, burglary is a common event. Most of us have been – or probably will be – the victim of some criminal offence.

The majority of crimes are property offences. Someone steals something from another; perhaps money, a car, household belongings, or goods for sale in a shop. A disturbingly large number of violent crimes also occur, although they are a minority of the overall figures. Murder, rape, child abuse, and other brutal aspects of lawless behaviour happen on a daily basis. The victims are real human beings, not mere statistics. The hurt and suffering is occurring in every society. As traditional values have been breaking down and a less inhibited individualism has surfaced, an apparently civilised and peaceful country like England has increasingly seen horrific outbursts of violence. Recent instances of petrol being poured over someone and ignited are similar to the black tribal killings more commonly known in South Africa. Hospital casualty departments, especially those based within our inner city areas, have noticed an increase in savage attacks with machetes or other weapons that inflict maximum pain and which leave visible reminders.

The so-called property offences also result in human suffering, albeit in different ways to the atrocious crimes of murder, rape, and so on. Whereas rich people are usually able to quickly replace what has been stolen or vandalised, the less wealthy sections of society generally experience more prolonged misery and hardship. Improved security precautions and adequate insurance cover are bought at a cost, easily afforded only by those with plentiful financial resources. Small businesses, owned and run by hard-working individuals, are similarly affected in comparison with the larger companies which are more able to absorb the losses caused by crime.

Domestic burglary is often done by disillusioned and maladjusted young people who feel that society "owes" them. Breaking into another person's house is justified on the grounds that someone else has got more than them. Crime is seen as an apparently easy or alternative way to get what they want – and perhaps, if only through the gesture of committing the offence, getting "even". Offenders generally shut out any awareness of causing personal hurt to the owners of the property they steal. Yet terror, anger, bitterness, panic, frustration, fear, and anxiety are commonly felt by the victims of burglary. Old people are particularly frightened and often live in apprehension of what could happen. Children may wet their beds night after night following a break-in at their house. Your home is usually equated with privacy; to have this unexpectedly disturbed can be felt as an acute intrusion. Some burglars spitefully defecate and/or urinate on the carpets and beds of houses they steal from.

The majority of criminal actions happen because of a blatant disregard for others. Selfish considerations dominate and are expressed in obviously anti-social ways. Victims suffer as a result. Subtle long-term consequences also occur. Increased distrust and greater emphasis on self-protection are common, part of an overall hardening of attitudes.

iii. Substance abuse

To help cope with the high level of mental stress associated with modern lifestyles, many people turn to the use of various substances (legal and illegal) for relief. Some do so to block out specific unpleasant feelings or memories. When detrimental effects result, especially on a regular basis, this is symptomatic of substance abuse. This includes the excessive use of cigarettes, alcohol, anti-depressant

Indicators of suffering

medication, illegal drugs, and the improper use of various solvents such as glue-sniffing.

Medical experts began to realise the dangers of smoking in 1950. By the early 1960s, it had been established beyond reasonable doubt that this habit causes ill-health and death. Despite clear warnings on cigarette packets and up to £10 million a year being spent on health campaigns against tobacco use, about 12.5 million adults in the UK still smoke cigarettes. Almost a quarter of 15-year-olds – both boys and girls – are regular smokers, despite the fact it is illegal to sell cigarettes to children under the age of 16. Each year, approximately 115,000 smokers in the UK die prematurely as a result of their habit. That means 315 people daily, or one person every four and a half minutes. It is as if a jumbo jet crashed every day with no survivors. Before dying of lung cancer, heart disease, bronchitis, emphysema, etc, these people usually suffer intense discomfort. Smokers who smoke between 1 and 14 cigarettes a day have eight times the risk of dying from lung cancer compared to non-smokers; smoking more than 25 cigarettes a day increases the risk to 25 times greater, compared to non-smokers. Smoking also results in thousands of leg amputations each year due to peripheral vascular disease (poor circulation of the blood). In pregnant women, smoking leads to an increased risk of spontaneous abortion, premature birth, and under-weight babies. Passive smoking – breathing in other people's cigarette smoke – harms babies and children, as well as causing lung cancer deaths.

The tobacco industry spends over £113 million each year advertising cigarettes in the UK. (In the USA, the annual budget for cigarette promotion is over US$3000 million.) Many movie stars and television actors/actresses continue to portray smoking as part of the "cool" or "fashionable" image – and as an "acceptable" means of managing stress. Tobacco is the only legally available consumer product which kills people when it is used entirely as intended. The British general public are well educated, but millions still continue smoking knowing that it will probably kill them.

Even some doctors and nurses smoke. Why? Smoking costs the National Health Service in the UK £610 million a year for treating diseases caused by smoking.

27% of men and 11% of women in Great Britain exceed the sensible and safe amount of alcohol consumption according to government surveys. Misuse is even greater in young people. Excessive use of alcohol causes numerous social problems, as well as damaging health. Innocent people are killed or injured by drunk drivers who ignore the don't-drink-and-drive campaigns. The police catch over 100,000 drunk drivers each year – and there are many other offenders who don't get caught.

Christmas is traditionally a time for giving and caring. During a recent festive season, a boy was killed by a drunk driver. One year later, his brother still refused to visit the cemetery, unable to accept what had happened. His sister had a miscarriage – due to the trauma, according to her doctors. Three days after the killing, the boy's father took an overdose. As the mother explained, her family had been torn apart. The drunk driver got a fine and a suspended three month jail sentence.

Alcoholics themselves are of course suffering, although their habitual drinking partly hides the deeper problems. They may deny both their addiction and the need for help. Their families and close friends are also affected. Alcohol abuse can ruin careers. Working hours are lost, and accidents and bad decisions occur. Drunkenness might lead to the beating and sexual abuse of wives and children. Family breakdown is a common result. Alcohol is involved in one out of three cases of child cruelty and one in three divorce petitions.

Drug and solvent abuse is widespread in our society. We have more than 25,000 notified heroin and cocaine addicts in the UK. The actual number is estimated to be approximately five times what is known – making a probable total in excess of 125,000; (some believe the number to be much higher). Criminals are now targeting and supplying school children. Drug taking appears to be more common amongst young people than ever before. Some experts predict that we will shortly be in a situation where nine out of ten 16-year-olds will be taking drugs and/or dealing. Government spends hundreds of millions of pounds each year to tackle drug abuse in terms of law enforcement, deterrence, prevention, and treatment. Yet the problem is growing and seems likely to persist.

The wider cost of drug abuse is incalculable. Drugs can cause under-achievement at school and work, ruining lives. They can cause physical and mental injury, as well as death. Crimes of theft, fraud, and violence are often linked to drug addiction. Many addicts steal to finance their habit. The supply of illegal drugs is a thriving and well-organised international business, involving huge amounts of money. Drug dealers frequently use extreme violence to maintain their part of the market – threatening, injuring, and even killing rival gangs who attempt to "steal" their business. Officials are bribed. Innocent people who accidentally get in the way are treated mercilessly. Millions of customers, many dissatisfied with conventional society, continue to buy.....paying what can be a high price.

iv. Other addictions

Many people suffer through various other forms of addictive behaviour. Excessive shopping has got numerous individuals and families into severe debt. Reckless spending beyond the means of paying has become easy through the widespread availability of credit. Debt quickly spirals out of control. Anti-depressant drugs are used in extreme cases to help shopaholics suppress the urge to buy and buy. Perhaps such people are only the tip of an iceberg?

The eating disorders of anorexia nervosa and bulimia are now well-known. Anorexics develop an unhealthy obsession with losing weight to the point of endangering their lives. Invariably, it is a symptom of some deeper psychological trauma. Bulimia is slightly different, but equally self-destructive. It involves a cycle of uncontrolled bingeing, followed by purging through forced vomiting or laxative abuse. Both of these eating disorders, usually associated with teenage girls or young women (although not always), provide the sufferer with a means of self-control and thereby a form of short-term relief from the underlying problems. Such behaviour might be experienced as something powerful in the midst of more general feelings of helplessness and a lack of self-worth.

Self-abuse can manifest itself in further ways. Self-injury through hitting, burning, scratching, and/or cutting oneself is often done in secret. This physical self-harm is not usually linked with suicide. As above, it hides an unresolved dilemma. The process of cutting or hitting, like eating disorder behaviour, gives the individual a means of control and release through distraction. Self-abuse can also involve the repeated selection of abusive partners.

Less dramatic, but much more common, is the addiction to over-eating. Being overweight has become socially acceptable because many people in society are now on the plump side. The frequency of obesity has also significantly increased, but is still generally regarded as undesirable. Although the reason for a large proportion of society being overweight might be explained due to greater affluence and less physically active lifestyles, trying to cope with high levels of stress must also be a significant factor. Food is a readily available commodity, providing an easy method of suppressing or relieving anxiety. Comfort eating, especially when excessive, is frequently done in secret. Whereas an alcoholic might fool a group of strangers about his or her problems, a fat person cannot; obesity is blatantly obvious. As with alcoholics or heroin addicts, obese people are usually in denial about their situation.....at least with regards to what inner difficulties the over-eating is hiding. Medical evidence is likewise often disregarded.

Gambling, when obsessive, also wrecks lives. Families normally suffer. Money for paying bills usually gets redirected to playing the slot machines, backing the next horse, or buying more and more lottery scratch cards. The casual flutter has become compulsive. It is no longer a matter of fun. Debt often follows. Deceit, when considered necessary by the gambler, helps continue the obsession. Once again, parallels exist with other forms of pathological behaviour.

Less apparent, but no less real, is the fact that many people are addicted to money or power. On a general level, it is common for someone to suffer boredom through doing work they do not enjoy, year after year. Job satisfaction and a sense of purpose are readily sacrificed for the weekly or monthly pay-packet. Clock-watching might dominate the daily routine. You may dream of the weekend to come or the next holiday. Monday mornings signal yet another five days of tedious monotony, interspersed with the occasional bit of office gossip. Others become unhealthily absorbed in their work – which is often little more than an exercise in making money if objectively considered – perhaps neglecting their families or missing opportunities to make the world a better place. Some thrive on power. By dominating or manipulating those under their control, the need to face one's own weaknesses can be displaced and hidden.

v. The pain of broken intimacy and isolation

Intimate relationships are frequently hurtful and therefore a common indicator of self-orientated dysfunctional behaviour. People are initially attracted to each other. Bonding develops and perhaps the couple fall in love. But if and when the relationship changes, how do the two lovers then treat each other? With kindness and respect as they part company? Unfortunately, often with bitterness, acrimony, or even full of vengeful intent. Pride might be damaged and the fragile ego exposed. Poor communication skills deteriorate into a hostile slanging match. The failing relationship becomes a pressure cooker, intensifying a mixture of harboured resentments and feelings of inadequacy. Separation is generally a messy affair.

Where children are involved in a spiteful failed marriage, it is not uncommon for them to become pawns in a game of "me versus you". For example, a bitter ex-wife might frustrate access for her former husband to see the children as a tool of revenge. She may also poison the children's young and impressionable minds against their father, confusing her broken intimacy with the responsibilities of parenthood. Agonising no-win situations can result. The ex-husband might be torn between not wishing to perpetuate the children's distress through continuing to take part in the woman's callous game playing, but neither wanting to desert his beloved youngsters.

Much emotional agony is also caused by isolation. Large cities can be especially lonely places for someone on his or her own. If a person's social skills are poor, making friends and establishing intimate relationships can be difficult. The rest of society is not overly helpful. A few words by singer/songwriter Joan Armatrading sum up this painful situation of loneliness, as well as hinting at a solution:

> *Don't isolate*
> *If you see someone not dancing, it's your fault.*
> *Never is too late*
> *A dance, short-lived or long, is all that's needed.*

vi. Non-human suffering

Human selfishness not only causes suffering to humans, but also to domestic and wild animals. Additionally, the environment suffers as a result of greed and exploitation. These wider issues reflect our sick behaviour as much as what we do to each other.

Bullfights in Spain provide an entertainment spectacle for locals and foreign visitors alike – although, after the torment, the climatic outcome of a bloody death for the bull is always predictable. In other countries, such as South Korea, eating dogs is a common practice. Citizens of Japan continue to enjoy the high-priced meat of whales and dolphins. In Africa, big game hunting is flourishing. A guest of one private game ranch in Zimbabwe wanted to shoot a giraffe to add to his trophy collection; the property only had six giraffes, but a creature which was blind in one eye was selected to be shot. Here in the UK, fox hunting with hounds is still legal (although perhaps not for much longer). We are the beast which kills for kicks.

Approximately 700 million farm animals are slaughtered in Britain each year. Why? Because people like to eat their flesh and wear their skins. Others are transported overseas alive, destined for unregulated slaughter houses or cruel veal crates banned in this country. Millions of fish are hauled out of the sea, left to slowly die in the back of fishing boats. Seals are killed if they threaten *our* fish stocks.

Each hen kept in a battery cage has a living space smaller in size than the cover of a telephone directory. They are never able to flap their wings, stretch, or preen properly. There are no quiet places for them to lay their eggs. Many are de-beaked when young. Broiler chickens are reared for meat rather than for egg production. They are normally kept intensively, with tens of thousands of birds crammed together, until slaughtered a few weeks later. Turkeys are killed at between 12 and 26 weeks of age, depending on production requirements; their natural lifespan is approximately 10 years. The approach of Christmas is not a happy time for turkeys. Pigs are also usually intensively reared, primarily for bacon, ham, pork, and sausages. Yet pigs are intelligent animals. The myth that pigs are dirty is untrue; if given the opportunity, they normally enjoy wallowing in wet mud to cool down in hot weather and rid themselves of pests.

Even if conditions for animal welfare are improved and the rearing which takes place behind the closed doors of factory farms is banned, a fundamental issue still remains: is it ethical to kill animals just because people enjoy eating them? We should quietly reflect on whether meat-eating can be part of a genuinely caring society – remembering that one person's dinner might be another's pet dog or holy cow. Millions of healthy vegetarians worldwide adequately demonstrate the option of a meatless diet. As a personal test, could you leap on the back of a cow and slit its throat with a carving knife – or shoot it – then chop it up before doing the final cooking process? If you could not do the actual killing yourself, in a non-life-threatening situation, then perhaps it is cowardly and two-faced to let someone else do the butchery for you? You are probably a vegetarian-in-waiting.

We are conditioned by society about what is cruel and what is acceptable behaviour. Few people in Britain would condone the eating of dogs, but most will happily eat pigs. Yet both dogs and pigs are intelligent creatures which make fine companion pets. Have we clearly thought about this matter of what we eat and why, instead of just following the crowd? Is there hypocrisy in our attitudes towards the suffering of animals? If you get upset about fox hunting, bullfighting, the killing of whales, or the poaching of elephants for their ivory, do you take part in the slaughter of millions of cows and sheep as a consumer? Why is your variety of gaining pleasure through the exploitation of animals different from another person's? How many ethically-motivated vegetarians still wear leather shoes? (Even if you don't eat its flesh, an animal cannot live without its skin.)

The general approach to wildlife and the environment is no less hypocritical than society's two-facedness concerning domesticated creatures (pets and farm animals). People are beginning to understand the need for conservation and are now supposedly "environmentally aware", yet they continue to take and take and take – usually giving back little or nothing in comparison. The "I want more" consumerism continues, slightly adapted, but largely unchanged. Natural resources carry on being depleted. Wild places are still exploited, with further habitat destroyed or altered every day. Many common species are becoming uncommon. Rare species are becoming endangered. Extinction might follow. Nature's balance is upset. We know this, and yet we continue to compulsively shop and selfishly indulge. The human population is too large; it needs to be voluntarily stabilised and then reduced.

Almost all of the environmental degradation happens unseen by the majority of people. The overall loss does not happen overnight; it occurs gradually. As we constantly update our view of the world in which we live, the slow erosion of nature is hard to detect. If we visit a place 20 or 50 years later – or compare photographs of then to now – human re-shaping of our planet is much more noticeable. Billions of self-orientated humans are collectively causing massive damage to the planet on which we all live.

The above examples are just a tiny part of a huge amount of suffering. What we do to others, to ourselves, to our domesticated animals, and to wildlife and the environment is disgraceful. We need to change, unless we think that this suffering is somehow acceptable. We must realise that almost all suffering is the consequence of selfishness. It is not inevitable, because an alternative non-selfish strategy is available for us to choose. If motivation is required for people to shake themselves out of their general apathy – or, for those who think they are not apathetic, to make the sense of urgency still greater and the coverage of their concern much wider – awareness of suffering can provide a powerful indicator of what we need to do.

7
Tears are not enough.....

As every day goes by, how can we close our eyes
Until we open up our hearts
We can learn to share and show how much we care
Right from the moment that we start
Seems like overnight we see the world in a different light
Somehow our innocence is lost
How can we look away?
'Cause every single day we've got to help at every cost

We can bridge the distance
Only we can make the difference
Don't you know that tears are not enough
If we can pull together
We could change the world forever
Heaven knows that tears are not enough

Then if we could try, together, you and I
Maybe we could understand the reasons why
If we take a stand, every woman, child, and man
We could make it work
For God's sake, lend a hand!

"Tears Are Not Enough" by Northern Lights

A child dies of diarrhoea in the third world every eight seconds. It is 1996 – not 1896. These unnecessary deaths could easily be prevented by modern sanitation, health education, and oral rehydration salts (currently costing 6p per packet to make a 1 litre solution). Numerous other illnesses go untreated, causing untold suffering and premature death for millions, when simple and low-cost medical remedies have long ago been discovered. Countries such as Ethiopia and Sudan are just a few hours away by air; they are not on some distant planet. Whilst this obscene suffering goes on and on, people travel worldwide on holidays and business trips, want bigger houses and faster cars, and moan about petty dislikes and minor problems. Some countries have immense wealth and all the luxury that money can buy, whilst other countries remain poor and unable to provide even basic health care.

We live in a society where you can get fined for parking a car in the wrong place, possibly because this might cause some limited inconvenience to others – yet it is "acceptable" to ignore the fact that innocent children in the third world die every few seconds of easily treatable diseases. The news media will occasionally focus on the plight of a British child who requires a specialised life-saving operation or course of experimental treatment, perhaps being pioneered in the USA, with costs of anywhere between £75,000 and £200,000 – so why do the daily headlines not include "African children still dying unnecessarily!".....? The usual media response is that the story of third world poverty is not news; the same thing happens each day, so there is no new information to report! And the general public do not complain because their caring is equally limited; it is easier to avoid or ignore what is happening out of sight. But how would people feel if the situation was reversed? It would be different if it was the viewer's or reader's child dying unnecessarily because of the lack of a few pence worth of medicine, or the news editor's son or daughter.....

Our first spontaneous trip to Ethiopia during the height of the 1984/1985 famine concentrated on emergency relief. We were directed by the Ethiopian authorities to Makelle in Tigré, one of the worst hit areas, where at least 300,000 starving people had gathered in desperation. We mainly took blankets on this first occasion, which we had found out were a life-saving commodity. Tigré is a high mountainous area and the nights can be bitterly cold. Thousands of Ethiopian families were living just outside the tented relief camps without shelter, exposed to the harsh elements.

Already weakened by famine, hypothermia and pneumonia were commonly the final killers. The warmth of a simple blanket could literally make the difference between life and death, in addition to slightly easing the general suffering.

We personally distributed the relief goods ourselves, thereby making sure that everything was best used. On the final day of distribution, the last 500 blankets arrived from our base at Addis Ababa with the British Royal Air Force when we discovered that 5000 mothers – with their children – had been lined up to receive them. Someone had misheard or misinterpreted "500" as "5000", an understandable error in the circumstances. The situation was immediately explained to the waiting people and I promised to help those most malnourished or ill – limited to 1 in 10 of those assembled – even though every single family clearly needed urgent assistance. Incredibly, there wasn't one case of grabbing nor a single complaint. Instead, many of the mothers who did not receive a blanket joined those who did in kissing me on the hand in thankful appreciation – surely one of the most humbling experiences imaginable. How could the world be so unfair, with the "have's" in the rich countries being constantly dissatisfied, whilst the "have not's" in Ethiopia and elsewhere – the poorest of the poor – were grateful for something as basic as a blanket? How had the situation been allowed to get so bad, so disproportionate, and so desperate? Within all the complexity, the fundamental problem is simple: self-orientated behaviour.

Back in Sussex, England, after this first trip, many people praised our humanitarian effort. One local man expressed his thoughts at a small public gathering by commenting that few people could honestly say that they have saved the life of another human being. However, from my perspective, it would have been inappropriate to dwell on such praise when much more help for Africa was clearly needed. A decade later, I recently watched the film *Schindler's List*. It tells the true story of how a German businessman saved the lives of a thousand Jews during World War II, when they would otherwise have been killed by the Nazis during the mass extermination. When the day of liberation came, these thankful Jews made a commemorative ring out of gold teeth-fillings and presented it to Oskar Schindler as a token of their gratitude. Schindler immediately broke down on being given the gift, acutely conscious of how he could – should – have done more, thereby saving additional lives. It was a parallel situation to when I stood face to face with Ethiopian famine victims on the mountain plateau in Tigré. The often used expression of doing "a little bit" to help illustrates the current limits to human responsibility. We must do more – and keep on doing more – whilst such problems demand our attention. If someone is suffering unnecessarily, we cannot turn away. Tears are not enough.....

People in the third world countries frequently warm to the name of our aid charity: You And Me. They seem to quickly grasp the simple inclusive concept of everyone coming together to solve the problems of absolute poverty. As we were developing the medical clinic at Awad el Sid in Sudan during 1986, one of my many jobs was to build a raised brick path; the rainy season was beginning and we needed to link up the thatched mud huts which initially accommodated our work. It was morning and a number of patients were waiting in the clinic compound for their turn to be seen. One man started helping by passing the bricks to me, speeding up my task. He had advanced leprosy. Where ten fingers/thumbs had once been, he now only had short stumps coming out of the palms of his hands. This most disabled of the day's patients was the first to help – singing as he worked, which included three English words, You And Me, sung over and over again. Others quickly joined in, following his example. Nobody had taught this man with leprosy the usual strategy of making "I can't, because....." excuses. He clearly understood our simple, practical philosophy.

A common utterance which I have heard many times here in Great Britain and elsewhere, effectively reinforces the complacency of people closing their minds to the third world issue. It is usually politely expressed as a question: why do they have so many children? Sometimes a person will more bluntly state that third world poverty is the local people's own fault because of their high birth rate. Such statements reveal an unthinking ignorance. I usually reply by reminding the person of two points. Firstly, the birth rate is high in response to the high infant mortality rate – a situation which can be changed by providing basic health care facilities; family planning becomes a realistic and attractive proposition once medical treatment is available. Secondly, larger families are generally needed in a low-tech society; children's help is required for fetching water (often at some distance from the family home), for tending/harvesting crops, and they provide the equivalent of a pension for their parents' old age. The difficulty with most people, when faced with the issue of inequality between the "rich" and "poor" countries, is that they mentally search for an explanation to justify their inaction. Or else they merely agree that the situation is indeed appalling, but do little or nothing about it, perhaps mumbling expressions of being "powerless" or blaming "the government" for not doing more. In short, the majority of people will say anything as a way out of accepting their full share of personal responsibility. From an environmental point of view, it is people in the industrialised countries who are causing most of the damage; a family in a developed country consumes a much greater amount of natural resources than one living in a developing country.

One of the best songs of all time, written in response to the 1984/1985 crisis in Africa, must be *We Are The World*. Sung by a host of the music industry's celebrities under the name of USA for Africa, it followed Britain's *Do They Know It's Christmas?* and preceded the transatlantic Live Aid concert. The words helped stir the conscience of the developed countries. The song became a sort of unofficial anthem for You And Me, as it expressed so clearly our own feelings. A decade or so later, the plea for a more compassionate human race is still just as acutely relevant.

> *There comes a time when we heed a certain call*
> *When the world must come together as one*
> *There are people dying*
> *Oh and it's time to lend a hand*
> *To life – the greatest gift of all*
>
> *We can't go on pretending day by day*
> *That someone somewhere will soon make a change*
> *We are all a part of God's great big family*
> *And the truth you know love is all we need*

"We Are The World" by USA for Africa

The level of suffering which is happening today in the third world is unacceptable. But what about the future? Developing countries are eager to copy the developed countries. They are held spellbound by the possibility of economic prosperity.....by what money can buy. Generally, they only see the attractive side of industrialised societies. The negative elements – high levels of stress and dissatisfaction, crime, drug abuse, pollution and environmental exploitation, etc – are ignored or unnoticed. A basically simple "I want" attitude to life is quickly being replaced with the more compulsive "I want more" mentality. An alternative development path is therefore required. Developing countries need to critically look at the developed countries and learn from the mistakes as well as the better side of progress. If this does not occur, one lot of problems will merely be replaced by another set.

8

A waste of money....a waste of life

At the beginning of the last chapter, I drew your attention to the fact that a child dies of diarrhoea in the third world every eight seconds. Anyone who knows me, or who has read my previous book, or seen the dedication at the beginning of this one, will realise that this is not just a statistic. During my second trip to Ethiopia in 1985, the day before flying back to Britain, I travelled to the Wollo region in a Polish Air Force helicopter. That afternoon, in a remote village, a 15-year-old girl died in my arms. If I had had a few pence worth of medicine with me, I could have almost certainly kept her alive. Her death was unnecessary. I promised myself never to forget this girl whose name I never knew. It is an example which epitomises what is going so badly wrong in this modern age of plenty. We have the technology, the means of international communication and transportation, and the wealth to eradicate such things. There can be no excuse for what is still happening. This is more than just general poverty – it is an unacceptable waste of life.

There are many organisations working in the field of relief and development. These are mostly charities. Together with the relevant international government departments, the appropriate sections of the United Nations, and other specialist institutions, they assume responsibility for planning and implementing the humanitarian aid programme for the third world. People who work for the non-government organisations (NGOs) perhaps represent the healthier or more caring part of human behaviour, as these are the people who are making it their job to do something about the obscene suffering and gross inequality. Unfortunately, a lot is going sadly wrong. This chapter will highlight some of the ineffectiveness and inefficiency which is repeatedly occurring within the aid agency community. Once again, it illustrates the weakness and limitations of the self-orientated mind-set – even in a situation of apparent benevolent endeavour. I am sure that similar parallels exist in other areas of charity work.

Some people will not like me criticising charities. They may prefer to keep on believing that their donations are spent wisely, unwilling to face the harsh truth of sloppy wastefulness and even outright deceit. Giving to charity for many people is partly a way of easing their conscience – so, by discussing the ineffectiveness and inefficiency of these organisations, there is an automatic link to uncomfortable personal feelings and avoidance. A few might even say that I am being "negative", but they would be denying the need for truthfulness and constructive criticism. Others will welcome such openness, which may confirm their own existing suspicions. From my perspective, I hope people will try to be open-minded and able to face the testimony of direct experience – but without becoming cynical to the point of not doing anything. Do not live in a make-believe fantasy world, nor cut off from real suffering. Instead, think about what is going on and work for change through reforming what is currently wrong.

Aid agencies generally exaggerate the amount of good they do and gloss over their failings. Aid has become a massive international "business", with most organisations energetically empire building and keenly flying their own flag. Competitiveness is rife. Big charities especially have become a law unto themselves. The world of aid agencies is often far apart from the realities of being poor. Expatriates can be extraordinarily arrogant towards the local people. It is not uncommon for the wrong kind of aid to be provided. "Sustainability" of projects is usually a concept restricted to funding applications and report writing. Intelligent-sounding jargon hides a mass of practical incompetence. There is too much bureaucracy and unnecessary administration, even within the NGOs.

Actions Speak Louder Than Words

The main problem, of course, is the staff themselves. They operate from the same ordinary consciousness as almost everyone else. The usual self-orientated considerations persist and so spoil the pure spirit of charity. It is normal (and therefore "acceptable") to want this and that for yourself – and to want security for your organisation. But this dilutes what can be done for the intended beneficiaries. Such self-orientated charitable expenses are invariably justified in some way. There is always enough money for staff salaries, posh offices, and to buy yet another new 4WD vehicle. But the things which they tell you are most needed – such as basic medical drugs for health care – are frequently in short supply. Money is wasted on non-essentials. As an indicator of misspending, the organisation which I most respect in some ways has been recently asking for donations of £2 per month. Their fund-raising campaign material powerfully describes several ways in which this small amount of money could help the poorest of the poor – *if it was spent directly according to need.* What the appeal information does not tell you is that the director has a salary of approximately £50,000 a year and that the UK-based staff's annual wages cost over £18.5 million. Not to mention all the many other self-orientated expenses. This charity is not unusual.

For over a decade, You And Me has practically demonstrated a better way. Myself and others here in the UK have worked unpaid, financially supporting ourselves part-time, putting our charity commitments first. (Our Sudanese, Ethiopian, and Eritrean staff are paid according to local wage levels, as alternative part-time work is generally unavailable in the remote villages overseas. Other aid agencies, in contrast, usually pay much higher salaries than we do, resulting in "staff poaching" between the organisations and from local government departments, etc.) I am not a casual volunteer, but rather a non-paid professional. Poor by British standards, in certain ways I am still a millionaire when compared with average third world hardships. It is good that charities have become more professional in their methods of working during the past 50 years or so – but real professionalism has little to do with whether or not a person is paid. It is the various appropriate skills and other qualities which are important. Charities need to progress further by enlisting non-paid staff with professional skills or else restricting wages to subsistence levels only. A change towards this approach would at first be resisted, as few staff are likely to welcome the loss of money for themselves. Current entrenched assumptions and expectations need to be vigorously challenged. Personal sacrifices have to be made, but are more than worth it for what can be achieved as a result. By beginning this shift of attitude in such a radical and personal manner, it is probable that most other mental cobwebs could then be more easily blown away. Avoidance tends to breed avoidance; freshness of attitude can likewise be infectious. The money that could thus be saved on wages alone, to use the above example of a single charity's UK-based staff, would be more than enough to run an extra 600 medical clinics – each able to examine, diagnose, and treat 35,000 patients a year.

Communication between NGOs is inconsistent. Aid agencies have been described as "a nest of vipers". Bitching, jealousy, snobbishness, and elitism all form part of this NGO rivalry. Divisions are created, causing mixed levels of co-operation. Unnecessary mistakes and duplications occur. Willingness to work in certain remote areas is sometimes influenced by seeing which other organisations have already agreed to do so – or perhaps determined by available facilities for staff; humanitarian needs do not always come first. Project commitment is often too short-term. Funding grants encourage quick spending, rather than careful spending. Frequent staff changes upset project management and implementation, as different people generally bring with them their own style of approach. Expatriates rarely stay long enough in any one place to achieve genuinely sustainable results; NGO "tourists" are common. Misfits easily find a place within the staff of aid agencies, as standards are less rigorously enforced overseas. Racial and religious prejudice is widespread.

Actions Speak Louder Than Words

When expatriates or city-based nationals are recruited to work at field level, any initial novelty or idealism quickly wears off. As life is usually seen as easier and more luxurious at head office, the self-absorbed urge to win promotion soon takes over. A management job thereby becomes preferable to remaining as a field worker and the race is on to climb up the ladder. Field visits by senior staff are often too short – perhaps lasting only a few hours or a couple of days at the project site – as city-based individuals might be unwilling to adapt to simpler living standards. Thoughts and feelings of unfairness between staff at field level and head office can result in frustration and poor communication. "Red carpet" visits by VIPs are usually little more than a public relations exercise. Real problems are often ignored or just mentioned in passing, with the emphasis being on producing a positive impression. These "feel good" events disrupt working practices, wasting time and resources.

Surveys and project evaluations should be helpful, but may actually prove to be merely an intellectual exercise – meaningless in practical terms. Thoroughness, frank honesty, and sound application are commonly absent. Quantity is often used to disguise the lack of quality. Project inputs are highlighted to measure achievement, which can be grossly misleading. Big annual budgets become status symbols between NGOs and more generally within the wider aid community, together with the newness and sophistication of their 4WD vehicles. Funding grants follow fashionable theories. Superficial accountability hides fiasco after fiasco, widespread mediocre performance, and even corruption. (A Sudanese government official in Khartoum once commented to two of You And Me's nurses: "It's nice to be working with a non-corrupt organisation!") Failure is frequently forgotten as quickly as possible. Individuals progress in their NGO careers without the pressure to demonstrate real project success or practical ability. Playing the image game and being good at report writing are qualities more regularly seen. The aid industry has moulded itself by conditioned imitation. Bad habits are duplicated

A waste of money....a waste of life

and glossed over, time after time. Mediocrity and self-preservation leads to a lack of incentive to make radical changes. The disparity between well-paid NGO expatriate staff and the poor people who are in need of help – or the interior of a charity's head office compared to the inside of an African mud hut – says it all.....and suggests where most of the donated money is spent.

On a lighter but still serious note, one of the funniest instances of inappropriate aid being sent overseas happened in response to the Bangladesh floods of 1988. A shipment of bras arrived for distribution. Most of the staff were nonplussed by this strange consignment, but one person came up with a good use for the bras; they were used as measuring scoops for distributing rice to the flood victims!

The following example illustrates the need for more careful selection of staff. A project supervisor in Ethiopia quickly noticed that things were going wrong. One of the NGO's employees seemed to be especially unsatisfactory. The supervisor – a mature and thoughtful Scandinavian farmer – decided to have an informal talk with this individual, as a first step towards trying to improve the situation. When asked about his previous work experience, the employee openly volunteered that he had been an executioner for Idi Amin in Uganda! He candidly admitted disposing of up to 20 people per day and showed no guilt or regret about his former job. He had since been working for this religious NGO for about 10 years. All the expatriate project officers during this time had apparently failed to enquire about his past; nor did they seem to have bothered themselves about the Ugandan refugee's poor current job performance and how this was having a disrupting influence on the overall project.

Wastage of funds and general incompetence are the biggest problems, but there can also be a more sinister aspect to why aid fails to reach those in desperate need. Expatriate staff are sometimes involved in illegal activities, cold-heartedly exploiting their humanitarian positions. I have personally witnessed aid workers packaging up valuable antiques for smuggling back home, and seen others trading with local villagers in precious stones. I have investigated cases of blatant project misuse and gold smuggling, and heard confidential testimonies of NGO staff who have observed their own colleagues or those in other organisations stealing large amounts of money from the overseas budgets.

The intended beneficiaries of aid – the poorest people in our world – are largely voiceless and at the mercy of the various charities, UN agencies, and governments. The local people are not always consulted, and community involvement might not be encouraged. The aid industry is generally self-absorbed and full of its own importance. Donors' money – and public tax – is given to help relieve suffering.....not to fund the careers of hundreds of thousands of aid workers. The needs of the poor must always be paramount – not the self-orientated wants of an organisation and its staff. Everyone capable of reading this book has a responsibility for what is going on. Searching questions have to be asked and re-asked. Answers should be carefully examined and challenged. Most charities have an extremely slick presentation, employing people well-trained in public relations. Do not be fobbed off by the clever use of words and statistics. (If you have learned to generally doubt the intentions and performance of politicians, why not also the staff who self-promote and defend the agendas of charities?) Think about who is really gaining. Who is looking after who? You – the people who directly or indirectly fund the aid programmes – must demand change. Due to their vested interest, it is doubtful that the aid agencies will change easily. Few people within these organisations are likely to instantly respond in a positive manner, eager to give up their comfortable salaries and new 4WDs. Most will probably resist change and attempt to justify their decisions. Like cornered rats, they can be expected to fight. They will do so with cleverness and professional skill. Do not be deterred if you care about those who need the aid. Charitable organisations need to be reminded about the integrity of purpose inherent in the true spirit of charity.

SECTION THREE:
WHY IS IT SO DIFFICULT TO CHANGE?

9
Conditioning

The film *Awakenings* is based on a true story. Dr Malcolm Sayer began working in a hospital for the chronically sick in the Bronx, New York. Some of the seriously disabled cases in his care were post-encephalitic patients - people who had suffered inflammation of the brain earlier in life. During the summer of 1969, Dr Sayer "awakened" these chronically sick patients, beginning with Leonard Lowe who had been "asleep" for 30 years. In the *Awakenings* movie portrayal of these events, the recently "awakened" Leonard (played by Robert De Niro) expresses his fresh perspective on life after reading a newspaper, which he has noticed contains nothing but bad news. Leonard realises that people have forgotten the value of life. He sees that people need to be reminded of this - to be reminded of the wonderment of life and what it is to be alive. Dr Sayer (played by Robin Williams) agrees that we do not really know how to live.....

People have described my enlightenment as a massive awakening from the dream of normal or ordinary consciousness. This dream or blinkered state of limited awareness is caused by and perpetuated through psychological conditioning. Generation after generation, throughout the world's human population, people have learned to put their own self-interests first. Each individual develops a unique variation of the self-orientated strategy from childhood to adult life. This strategy is based on partly getting what you want and partly on self-defence considerations.

Children quickly learn how to manipulate others in order to get what they want. They build up a complex pattern of behaviour in response to the adults and other children with whom they interact. If a child is shown love and caring, and encouraged to express himself or herself as a worthwhile member of the family or group, this should result in a level of development which is basically healthy and balanced. However, if a child's thoughts and feelings are frequently discouraged or denied, this set of experiences will probably produce a less healthy, more problematic type of development.

Some families are exceptionally psychologically immature and therefore regularly dysfunctional. They probably have extreme negative feelings towards themselves and/or others, resulting in various anti-social relationships. However, the vast majority of families display average behaviour. Personal inadequacies may frequently reveal themselves through minor problems and occasional major upsets, or else there might be a strong emphasis on conformity and maintaining a non-confrontational mediocrity. These mid-range families are mildly dysfunctional and lack real maturity; a superficial social politeness disguises an underlying insecurity and general mistrust of others. Then there are some families which, in comparison, are exceptionally well-balanced. These people are lovingly supportive, open-minded, and freely able to express themselves in a relatively honest and straightforward way. So, young children can learn a wide range of behaviour, usually primarily dependent upon the degree of psychological health or ill-health of the family setting in which they are brought up.

When a child starts attending school, the psychological conditioning process is intensified. The teachers may present different standards from those taught at home, causing the young child some confusion or conflict. If the child adjusts to

Conditioning

the values of school life, these might be partly unacceptable within the family group. This dilemma is usually resolved by the youngster adopting dual types of behaviour in an attempt to satisfy the expectations of both sets of adults.

Children are very influenced by what other children are doing. There is usually an initial sense of wanting to be accepted as part of some social group. This often involves developing behaviour that is agreeable to the peer group, but which is not necessarily always welcomed by others such as parents. Divisions and contradictions can easily occur as a result of these varying pressures. Increased social interaction also creates the challenge of competitiveness - with different potential outcomes, both healthy and unhealthy. Behaviour therefore becomes more and more complex, shaped by the child's assorted experiences and responses to these experiences. This childhood development process results in the individual identifying with - and being identified by - one or more of a series of social labels: good at schoolwork, shy, musically talented, a troublemaker, attention seeking, intellectual, good at sports, member of a gang, average, someone who is popular with everyone, one of the school bullies, a joker, a tell-tale, a dim-wit, and so on.

Adult hypocrisy is indirectly taught to young people, encouraging or sanctioning double standards. Recently talking about this type of conditioning to a group of school children, they all easily recognised this influence in their daily lives. One of the young people related it to the following incident. At school, the pupils had been told that a certain corridor was temporarily out-of-bounds due to adjacent class rooms being used for examinations. They were further instructed, both verbally and through written notices, to be quiet whilst near this particular area. However, as the young person had seen for himself, teachers continued using this out-of-bounds corridor.....speaking loudly to one another whilst walking along. If this "lesson" - teaching that it is okay to have double standards - can be picked up from authoritative figures in the place where we send children to learn, you can imagine what influences exist elsewhere in society.

Actions Speak Louder Than Words

The teenage years are often a difficult time. The onset of puberty brings further complications. Sexual urges prompt new emotions, which need to be incorporated with existing feelings and values. As well as opening up new considerations, these personal development changes may reinforce or threaten self-images that have already been formed. Perceptions of self-confidence and being likeable to others, and/or various inadequacies and fears, might arise or be heightened. At the same time, the teenager may be beginning to challenge figures of authority - parents, teachers, and perhaps grown-ups in general - as increased awareness and experience reveals adult hypocrisy. As self-identity continues to grow and the young person prepares to venture away from the family nest alone, yet more potential conflicts emerge. Different individuals have different expectations of how they would like young people to behave and what they would like them to do - pressures which can cause anxiety, reluctant compromise, and two-faced relationships.

The conditioning continues during adult life. Career prospects are highly influential. The type of job and how the individual acts at work may have a major impact on general behaviour. Family pressures are often felt even more acutely as a young adult, with feelings of obligation and guilt common. Conformity encourages various "supposed-to-be" patterns. Intimate personal relationships present a further powerful source of influence. And the proverbial mother-in-law may add yet another complication! By this stage, the developing individual is likely to be an emotional wreck in need of psychotherapy or else someone with a toughened exterior skin.

Many people therefore find it hard enough just to get by in life a lot of the time, let alone push back the frontiers of human potential. They are busy defending their vulnerability, as well as building what they want. Keeping up appearances in the "supposed-to-be" game is an ongoing struggle. Ideals are frequently compromised and dreams are usually left gathering dust on the shelf. Survival of the fittest still applies. An ecological jungle has been

Conditioning

swapped for a concrete/plastic jungle. Complex psychological conditioning has developed in addition to the biological influences. Some of these pressures are obvious, but others are much more subtle and so might go unnoticed. The grip is tight and widespread.

Society may at times question parts of this psychological conditioning, but the self-orientated foundation invariably goes unchallenged. Experience of life seems to reinforce the presumption that human nature is inherently selfish to one degree or another. People thus learn to function within these boundaries. The alternative of non-selfishness is rarely, if ever, considered. Little reliable information about such a radically different way exists - and even less on how to achieve it - thereby restricting life to within the range of normal consciousness. However, if people could take time out to look at what they had been automatically served up for consumption, it would be quickly realised that the plateful was a stomach upset waiting to happen; the menu would be quickly consulted for choice or another restaurant selected.

A sense of dissatisfaction or wanting to break out of traditional limitations is, of course, happening. Minority group protests are common. There is an increasing tendency towards greater individualism. A growing number of disenchanted people are seeking various alternatives, some seriously. Many good ideas have arisen and practical innovations realised. But - and here lies the snag or limitation - those individuals who have changed in some way merely end up creating a sub-culture, which may or may not become incorporated into mainstream society, still failing to burst the bubble of selfishness. The individual remains trapped by his or her image of separateness. And this is the fundamental problem. So the conditioning which prompts and reinforces normal consciousness continues in one form or another. There might be progress within the self-orientated boundaries, but the non-selfish alternative remains a largely unknown option.

10

Avoidance

Personal development through childhood and adult life is a journey which causes suffering, dilemma, and defensiveness. Traumas and misunderstandings occur. Painful experiences produce powerful lessons which are not easily forgotten. The individual is left with certain emotions which are uncomfortable and perhaps difficult to face. School didn't prepare you for having to deal with a broken love affair or suddenly being made redundant at work.

So traumatic memories of major and/or minor events are commonly hidden or veiled. Certain personal interactions are thereafter recognised as being potentially threatening and thus avoided. The open wounds and scars of previous hurtfulness might be denied - pushed away and neglected, perhaps festering - but they influence your ongoing behaviour. Added to these unique individual patterns of avoidance are the various constraints or taboos of the family group and also of society in general.

Some of this avoidance behaviour will probably not be clearly recognised by yourself, nor necessarily by others around you, due to the avoiding or defensive nature of such a strategy. Furthermore, it is common for people to select friends and acquaintances who are comfortable playing the same or a similar "supposed-to-be" game. Frequently, partners are likewise selected as mutual allies in the pretence. Subtle signals between people reinforce the "no go" areas of avoidance, helping to maintain a wall of silence. If the defences are blatantly threatened, this perceived danger may be met with immediate denial. It is hoped that by ignoring it, the problem will go away and therefore not exist.

If someone persists in rocking the proverbial boat, he or she is quickly shown disapproval and could be shut out or marginalised. In families, such non-conformist behaviour might produce arguments and eventually lead to the "offending" family member being labelled as "the black sheep". As people usually prefer to be accepted and liked by others, rather than called the odd-one-out or made outcast, the pressures are stacked in favour of a general tendency for avoidance being adopted as the normal practice. Playing the game, maintaining the status quo, is presented as the "safer" option; the straightforward alternative means facing awkwardness and insecurity, and is usually discouraged. In various ways, this mutual avoidance strategy provides the means for people to attempt to minimise their inner discomfort and suffering.

The avoidance or denial mechanisms are also used to shut off concern for the feelings of others, assisting self-orientated behaviour. The fact of numerous children in the third world dying every day due to the lack of a few pence worth of medicine is just one obscenity that goes on and on. Those living in the developed countries have the resources available to help if they really wanted to do so. But most people, most of the time, cut off to this horrendously unequal and unfair situation. Avoidance is the "easy" option - until, of course, it is yourself who needs help.

People have learned to care for themselves at the expense of caring for others. Cutting off allows someone to continue functioning selfishly, without too much concern or guilt - which would otherwise be hard to consciously bear unless the individual was prepared to change. Others appear more sensitive. But they usually bury their heads in the sand when the uncomfortable feelings get too much to handle. Some cannot even tolerate watching television pictures of starving famine victims - or animals being cruelly treated, or whatever - because they find it too painful. And so they turn away or switch off. But in comparison to the suffering of the real victims, such painful emotions are minor and partly perpetuated through indulgent self-pity. Avoiding reality may appear to be the easy short-term option, but it allows suffering to continue in the long-term. To be blunt, it is an immature and cowardly way of dealing with unpleasant situations; a better way for all demands to be found.

This same pattern of avoidance and/or denial can be seen to occur in attitudes towards the various organisations set up to bring relief to third world suffering or to help some other charitable area of need. The general public find it relatively easy to write out a cheque in the hope that they are doing something useful, avoiding widespread suspicions (probably including their own) that the majority of charities are wasteful at very least with regards to administration levels. Furthermore, if you try to tell them, some people do not want to hear that much of their donated money is misdirected or wasted. They will accept that the inefficiency and empire building tendencies go on, then shrug their shoulders with feeble excuses such as "But what can I do about it?" or console themselves with escapist platitudes like "What a shame! But at least we're doing a little bit to help. Not everything is wasted." All of which allows and encourages self-orientated behaviour to continue, along with the suffering. Third world poverty, cruelty to animals, etc etc may seem to be the problems which need solving - but the bigger problems which frustrate a solution, rarely recognised, are the inner psychological factors.

Avoidance is therefore a major part of the widespread normal conditioning. It is a lesson taught and learned by everyone to varying degrees. People influence each other as an on-going process. The manifestations of avoidance might be obvious or subtle.

One of the unfortunate personal consequences of avoidance is that it closes off part of your potential as a human being. You limit your sensitivity, appreciation, and compassion for life. You reduce your ability to give or respond to life in a fullness of relationship. You may not even be in touch with your true feelings. Whatever the degree, their expression will be restricted in some way. All this makes you less than your true potential. As well as directly or indirectly adding to the suffering of others.

Avoidance

Caught between the "I want" of desire and a capacity for compassion, life can seem like a complex puzzle. What do you do? Which way of behaving is right? Is there a balance? It is easy to get confused, unsure of how to handle and express these two contradictory sets of feelings. Some cope better than others. Some never become properly aware of the need to resolve this dilemma. Some passionately want to, but struggle in finding the means to do so.

To mask, minimise, or shut off your ability for pure caring, you will rationalise (or perhaps it would be more honest to say irrationalise) your chosen actions. This is the end result of the avoidance mechanism. By justifying a certain response, you can close the door on the feelings which prompted the need to choose. Sometimes forgetfulness may conveniently help you put off making any change. Or else the justifications might take the shape of an "I can't, because....." excuse. Or complacency could rescue you from having to make a decision, perhaps in the form of rationalising to yourself that things aren't that bad after all. In the next three chapters, we will consider further these common mechanisms of avoidance: forgetfulness, excuses, and complacency.

11

Forgetfulness

One of the major threats to the spark of new awareness is forgetfulness. A fresh insight, unless quickly reinforced and so stabilised, is likely to be dimmed by forgetfulness within a short time. It might even fade to nothing other than a blurred or distant memory.

We usually think of forgetfulness as being the absence of a particular memory. When is so-and-so's birthday? Which year did man first walk on the moon? What else do I need to get from the supermarket? This type of forgetfulness is more a matter of failing to remember certain facts and figures. Several techniques, such as using association and imagery, can greatly assist people to more easily harness the power of memory; necessary and useful information can thus be readily recalled.

It would be totally impractical to remember everything. Who needs to know what they have eaten for every meal on each day of their life? Or the names of everyone they have ever met? We retain mainly the information which is most beneficial or interesting to us. Sometimes we use diaries to help organise and remind our memory for the days and weeks ahead. Mostly, we forget. This is especially true in the modern world where our senses are continually being bombarded with all kinds of messages or input. We are surrounded by advertising, for example, which seeks to persuade us to buy this or that.

The type of forgetfulness which dulls sensitivity and dims any fresh awareness could be described as a care-less forgetfulness. It may occur unintentionally, or due to a deliberate unwillingness to change. When forgetfulness is unintentional - i.e. happening out of an automatic return to the same habitual patterns - it does so as a result of inattentive mindlessness. The increased awareness fails because it is not secured through being properly incorporated into the

Forgetfulness

existing framework of thoughts, feelings, values, etc. The person does not realise that an insight is likely to slip from memory if not stabilised. Forgetfulness may also occur more or less deliberately when any primary doubts or indecisions are not resolved concerning the consequences of the new realisation. There could be a conflict of yearnings, whereby you either settle for a half-hearted compromise or perhaps decide to take the course of least resistance. In these instances, the forgetfulness is based on ignore-ance. Where there is some difficulty, conflict, or inconvenience, it is easier to forget than to remember. You may say you want to change, but then actually prove unwilling to pay the price. You want this and you want that. You want to have your cake, but also to eat it. If the conflicting situation remains unresolved, forgetfulness gets you off the hook; you effectively select what you want to remember and so the subsequent vagueness of recollection can be said to be deliberate.

The following is a common example of this intentional forgetfulness. Two people meet and fall in love. Difficulties then occur and a separation follows. Original feelings change and the former lovers each find new partners. One or both may deal with the pain involved in ending the relationship by forgetting that they ever loved the other. The option of remaining open-hearted through the disappointment of failure is thus denied or avoided. Awareness is distorted and limits are self-imposed.

Freedom of choice allows us to forget when we want to forget. Sometimes this is genuinely helpful; on other occasions, it might be restricting a fullness of relationship with life. Selective memory can allow us to focus on what most needs to be done, or it can provide a means of escape for someone who is weak-minded and unwilling to face reality. Unhealthy forgetfulness generally occurs according to the individual's particular defences. An expanded awareness will only survive when sustained by being taken seriously by the person concerned. Like a new-born baby, it will thrive if given nourishment.

12

Excuses

When it comes to avoidance, people can suddenly become incredibly creative. Excuses roll off the tongue as easily as water off a duck's back. To get off the hook, someone will wriggle as strongly and persistently as an eel. Common sense and reason usually fade into the background, with the desire to avoid becoming all-important. Values normally held are ditched if they clash with the defence/escape strategy. It is avoidance at any cost.

Pick an issue. Third world suffering, for example. You tell others about what is happening, including the children who are dying unnecessarily. They agree with you that the situation is intolerable. Perhaps they show a genuine tear or two of emotion. But then you get realistic and practical. You ask these others what they are going to do - really do - in light of this conversation and heightened awareness/concern. At which point, watch out for a dramatic change of attitude. They will now probably shift from being in agreement with you to a more hostile, defensive position. The "I can't, because....." excuses will begin. Expressions of helplessness and ignorance will be offered as a poor excuse for inaction. If you challenge these hollow justifications, more will be invented. Personal responsibility is often nowhere to be found.

In an organised discussion about the need for non-selfish consciousness, I brought in the issue of third world poverty and the unnecessary deaths. It was immediately obvious to me that most of this group, who had apparently come to learn from my talk, were well practised in avoiding reality. Mostly members of the "spiritual circus", their idea of spirituality was not mine. Defensiveness came pouring out like a swarm of angry bees, more than I have seen before or since. So I kept hitting home with more and more indisputable harsh facts of life - which the avoiders kept trying to brush away. One usually kind-hearted woman finally said in a sweet-sounding voice: "Perhaps these people were meant to die." I have heard some astonishing excuses over the years, but this had to be a record breaker. Would this same individual have such blind acceptance of fate if one of her own children was seriously ill and in need of emergency attention? How would she feel if the surgeon wandered off to have a cup of tea or a game of golf in the middle of performing an operation, leaving the life of the woman's child to fate? "If he's meant to live, he'll still be alive tomorrow morning and I'll finish the surgery then....." would hardly be an acceptable response. In making her ridiculous statement, the woman conveniently forgot her belief in the freedom of choice. Weeks later, in retrospect, she expressed surprise at her reaction and what was within her.

The above bizarre attempt to avoid responsibility by resorting to the dubious metaphysical excuse of fate is an unusual example of a blame statement; more commonly, someone or something tangible is selected as a convenient scapegoat. The "I can't, because....." excuses use negative reasoning to justify personal inaction, whereas blame statements transfer the cause and/or solution of a problem onto someone or something else. The "if/but" excuses also displace accountability elsewhere. Continuing our usual example of third world suffering, "if/but" excuses might include the following statements: "But the government should do more." "What about the United Nations and all the charities?" "If the local people didn't have so many babies....." Switching examples, such as the case of a badly behaving child, parents might blame "the school", "the teachers", "other children", "television", "the neighbourhood" - but not themselves.

Consider the following story:

A man who had achieved the power of mind-over-body was challenged to prove his unusual abilities. The test was to spend a night naked at the top of a snow-covered mountain.

With only a book to read and a candle to see with, the man succeeded in demonstrating his resilience to the cold.

Next day, the challenger questioned the man, unwilling to accept defeat. "Did you have nothing to keep you warm?" "Nothing except my mental determination," the man honestly replied. "Not even so much as a candle?" "I had the light of a candle to read with." "So you failed the test!" exclaimed the challenger, obviously pleased with himself.

A few days later, the man invited his challenger to supper. After several hours of interesting conversation, the hungry guest could wait for food no longer and asked when they would eat. Our man, the host, immediately got up, saying "We'll go to the kitchen and see what's happening." Inside the kitchen, they saw a large cauldron of water for making a vegetable stew, with a candle underneath. The water was still cold. "It's not ready yet, although I've had it going all day."

Excuses hold you back from learning. The old is continually reinforced. Awareness becomes selective or stunted. You hear what you want to hear, and see what you want to see. Anything threatening your "safe" view of life is thereby controlled and usually avoided. This makes it difficult to grow in a healthy, balanced way. Reality is distorted. Evasion develops into being a friend, when it is actually an enemy. Excuses justify inaction, when you should be giving. Excuses prolong and sanitise selfishness.

13

Complacency

Avoidance allows you to cut off to what is difficult or painful to face. A series of excuses or justifications help you to rationalise the care-less decision. You argue for your limitations and defend them. This produces a degree of self-satisfaction. A "safe zone" is created, with threats minimised so long as you stay within the boundaries. Some people want the safety of a predictable routine. Others escape a fullness of relationship with life in more adventurous and apparently care-free ways. Whatever the level of avoidance or the means of self-satisfaction employed, the result is a state of complacency.

The majority of those searching for that "something more" are hampered by this problem of complacency. There might be a wish for greater awareness, but this is usually offset by the habitual desire for avoidance. Therefore, the searching becomes conditional. When the quest for that "something more" is originally sparked off, there invariably exists a genuine intention to change. But this freshness of spirit is quickly compromised by the old tendencies to avoid. Other-worldly belief options, with little or no need attached to face harsh current affairs, often present an easy and safe way forward. The searching thus develops an element of escapism – a flight of fancy, away from reality. A contradiction is created. There is open-mindedness towards what might be, but also evasion of what is actually happening. When someone points out this avoidance of reality, denials or excuses promptly follow so as to preserve the pretence.

It is not just the seekers of spirituality whose "open-minded" search becomes conditional. Even most scientists – the supposed standard-bearers of objectivity – are guilty of selling their ideal short. Science aims to be the pursuit of knowledge for its own sake; pure objectivity. Yet often the scientific method is reduced to becoming the tool of some lesser purpose. Instead of boldly exploring the wild jungle, scientific investigation is usually little more than a plant hunting trip to find new additions for an orderly garden. Within this botanical garden, where every specimen is identified and labelled, the scientist can stroll untroubled – secure in his or her knowledge that everything neatly fits, yet open to further species being discovered. This less challenging approach makes such matters as research funding and career building much easier to achieve. But the motivation and/or scope of the searching has changed. The wildness of the jungle has been ignored by focusing on the safety of a botanical collection. The pure ideal of science has been compromised.

There must, of course, be order in our lives. Otherwise, there would be unstructured chaos. But too often an incomplete system goes unchallenged. This attitude results in complacency, which is characterised by mental lethargy. Complacency occurs when someone neglects to try to gain increased awareness, neglects to stabilise any new awareness, and/or neglects to act on the awareness.

Complacency towards the suffering of others might be summarised by the smug contentment of the phrase "I'm alright, Jack!" When expressed in this way, the root cause of selfish preoccupation is obvious. The same inertia can also be seen in instances of personal suffering when an individual wallows in his or her own self-pity, rather than trying to work out a solution to the trouble. More often, however, complacency is subtle. The lack of forward progress might be disguised by movement of a sideways nature. Non-essential or less important activities hide an avoidance to do what is really needed.

The stagnation or lazy-mindedness of complacency can be countered by serious determination. Consistent effort is required. The need to overcome this state of apathy is especially important at the beginning. Otherwise, it is easy to never really get going – frustrated perhaps through

Complacency

delaying an initial decision, or by making half-hearted commitments which at best will lead to a stop-go-stop-go situation.

If you decide to attempt the shift towards non-selfish consciousness, you will need to relax the grip of avoidance. There must be a willingness to change the present circumstances to something genuinely different. Which means over-coming the quagmire of complacency. If you are not prepared to think, feel, and act in a new and determined way, then you will not change – other than through getting older and more experienced. Complacency and the other shackles of avoidance will remain. Real progress does not magically happen; it takes commitment and decisiveness to give the opportunity a chance to work.

14

The "I want more" mentality

Self-orientated consciousness is dominated with the "I want" or "I want more" mentality. Selfish desire usually preoccupies someone's life. It might be the desire for money, for possessions, for a better home. It might be the desire for power, for status, for influence over others. It might be the desire to be safe, to be comfortable, to be loved. It might be the desire for revenge, for control, for healing. It might be the desire to escape, to be happy, to be immortal. It might be the desire to travel, to be adventurous, to rebel.

Desire is self-indulgent. You want something and, when you get it, this produces satisfaction. For a while. Until you want again. Desire is an endless cycle. Your level of desire, compared to someone else's, might not seem extreme nor abnormal. But, in comparison with the way of non-selfishness, all desire is an unquenchable egotistic appetite. It is a restricted ambition, usually limited to what you want for yourself and your family. This "I want" or "I want more" mentality ignores the well-being and dreams of the whole.

There is a difference between the basic needs of life and the selfish wants of desire. For example, you need food to live. But this essential requirement usually becomes intertwined with the extra non-essential consideration of what you want, through having a range of available choices. So you might choose to eat meat, because you like its taste, even though it involves killing an animal just for your pleasure. This is not a true need, demonstrated by the millions of people who live healthily on a vegetarian diet. It is the greed of "I want". Sometimes greed turns excessive and an individual over-eats, perhaps to the detriment of their own health.

The "I want more" mentality

Through the mechanisms of avoidance, people often fail to perceive the difference between genuine needs and the non-essential wanting of desire. In this blurred confusion, people thus say "I need this and I need that" – when they are really talking about their wants. As society encourages the "I want more" mentality, it is hardly surprising that the level of general expectation is much higher than just receiving the basic needs for life and a few occasional treats. We are conditioned to be dissatisfied with the essential minimum to sustain body and mind. We are urged to want more.....much more. Mutual selfish desire is regarded as normal. It only becomes unacceptable behaviour when someone goes too far by breaking society's rules, such as in the case of one individual stealing the possessions of another. It is socially acceptable to want expensive clothing, luxury holidays, fast cars, etc etc, in a world where millions of other human beings are malnourished and dying from the lack of basic resources. The sense of true priority has been numbed by self-orientated desire. Objectivity has been clouded by the subjective "I want" considerations.

The "I want" strategy of desire does not produce constant happiness. To begin with, there is a heightened feeling of anticipation which usually stimulates initial pleasure and a sense of purpose. But when a desire is unfulfilled, it then causes disappointment, frustration, and perhaps a degree of bitterness. In more extreme instances, it can lead to depression and severe inner turmoil. If the desire is achieved, however, the resulting enjoyment or satisfaction is often short-lived and sooner or later fades away. The prospect of emptiness or boredom quickly prompts a new object of desire to be selected. And so the endless cycle continues over and over again. It is a cycle of "ups" and "downs". A person therefore attempts to maximise the enjoyable "ups" and minimise the depressing "downs".

The "I want" or "I want more" strategy produces a range of "winners" and "losers". This occurs because some are more successful at getting what they want than others.

People therefore learn through experience to adjust their ambitions and expectations accordingly. But the same basic reliance on desire for motivation continues, whatever its degree or mode of expression. Desire is a rudimentary part of self-orientated behaviour, providing the individual with a means to function. No radically alternative option is clearly known to people, other than a vague idea of some higher desireless spiritual state. Thus, there is no real choice available which can offer a practical and achievable substitute to the way of desire. There are just choices pertaining to the level and means of achieving desire. So the "I want" or "I want more" mentality continues.

Desire might be obvious or subtle. But it has become habitually addictive. Although there is a beginning and an end to the cycle of wanting and getting – or, if unsuccessful on a particular occasion, wanting and not getting – most people keep repeating this process time after time.....rather than sincerely and intelligently considering if there is another way. A lifetime of repetition does not make it easy to change or break out of the on-going routine. This fundamental attachment to desire is therefore a major difficulty.

15
Half-full or half-empty?

Another common difficulty to overcome is the tendency to compare up. This is also part of the general avoidance strategy. It helps you to focus on what is suitable for achieving your selfish wants, ignoring other considerations. It is frequently a subtle manoeuvre which you might be unaware of employing. Comparing up has usually become an automatic knee-jerk reaction to possible threat or criticism and might be used in conjunction with making an excuse.

Two colleagues personally wrote to an aid agency – actually one of the more open charities – having received an appeal letter asking for a regular donation of £2 per month. (The example of this organisation was referred to in Chapter 8.) They asked several questions in a straightforward and sincere manner, including how much the director was paid. The replies included a lengthy statement of justification, as well as the requested information. It was explained that paid staff get less than they could earn commercially – yet the charity also had to take into account what level of salary suitably skilled people could get elsewhere. It was also pointed out that there could be no comparison with some of the huge pay awards made to some directors in both the public and private sectors; (a current affairs topic at the time). Furthermore, one of the replies stated that their director was paid less than several heads of other charities of comparable size and influence. It must be said that this particular organisation has undoubtedly shown an above-average degree of thoughtfulness and intelligence in forming its policies (and perhaps also a certain amount of slickness in its presentation). But it is still comparing up. In justifying a salary of approximately £50,000 for its director and a collective cost of over £18,500,000 for paying its UK-based staff, the charity uses normal benchmarks. These reference points bear no relation to the third world situation which the charity is trying to improve, nor to the information presented to potential donors in the charity appeal letter which emphasises how £2 could make a difference to the poorest of the world's poor. Blatant double standards therefore continue to apply, despite the organisation's motto of "working for a fairer world".

The "I want more" mentality encourages this tendency to compare up. In its more obvious forms, the self-orientated inclination is frequently noticeable when someone wants the same material possessions as someone else; a neighbour's new car, for example, may cause envy and dissatisfaction. Instead of perceiving what might be half-full in your life and being content, you are likely to see it as half-empty. So "enough" is usually never "enough". The selfish ambition of wanting to be amongst the "have's" either prevents or limits concern for the "have not's". It distorts an objective view of life.

The Band Aid song *Do They Know It's Christmas?* highlighted the difference between rich and poor during the 1984/1985 famine. Acknowledging "our world of plenty", the lyrics honestly exposed the tendency to compare up, so as to prompt a caring and involved response. The line

> *Tonight thank God it's them instead of you!*

is especially powerful, followed by

> *And there won't be snow in Africa this Christmas time*
> *The greatest gift they'll get this year is life.*

Mention the subject of vegetarianism to a meat-eater. A common reaction will often be "But I don't eat as much meat as I used to....." – which is an apologetic excuse using the tactics of comparing up. Try telling a cow or a lamb that you want to eat one of its legs instead of its whole body; the animal will not be impressed by your logic, nor by your sincerity. A more straightforward self-assessment might be: "I really think meat-eating is selfish and cruel, but I enjoy

Half-full or half-empty?

doing it." Or, even better: "I'm aware of being hypocritical and need to change."

Comparing up reinforces avoidance, keeping you stuck in the same habitual patterns. By reducing the tension of some impending threat, you are able to maintain the status quo or regain the impression of safety. However, such a strategy denies the possibility of true openness. Comparing up facilitates self-orientated desire, allowing you to want what you haven't got – at the expense of being fully aware of and concerned for those worse off than yourself. You might greedily moan about not having more money, when many get by on much less. It is a matter of interpretation. How should you assess what is an appropriate choice of action? It is a question of half-full or half-empty?

16

The burden of responsibility

Most people's willingness to be responsible is half-hearted and they are often quick to suspend their own judgement – other than on a superficial level – if someone else is prepared to assume responsibility. This weak-mindedness was powerfully illustrated by a series of psychological experiments conducted at Harvard University during the early 1970s. The subjects believed they were taking part in a learning experiment. Each was given a list of questions to ask another person who was located unseen in an adjoining room connected by microphone. If this second person got an answer wrong, the subject had to press a button which gave an electric shock. In reality, the second person in the next room was an actor, employed to give an extremely convincing performance, and the apparatus and electric shocks were phoney. The subjects, however, did not know that the experiment was a set-up. They were told that with each successive wrong answer, the electric shock would become stronger.

The supposed "learning experiment" began well, with only mild electric shocks. However, as the test proceeded and the shocks became more powerful, the person in the adjoining room – i.e. the actor – started to cry out with pain and beg for the experiment to be stopped. This obviously worried the subject who was asking the questions and pressing the button which produced these apparently painful electrical shocks. It seemed clear from the screams and pleading that there was a real danger of serious injury or even worse. The subject protested to the experimenter about the level of distress being caused, indicating that the test should be stopped. But, each time, the subject was easily persuaded to carry on by the authoritative figure merely saying that a wrong answer had been given and that

The burden of responsibility

the experiment had to continue. Astonishingly, the subject was prepared to neglect his own sense of responsibility – transferring accountability for his part in the proceedings to the white-coated experimenter – and go on inflicting pain to another human being, even at apparently dangerous levels. Seeing film of these psychological experiments is a chilling reminder of how readily past atrocities must have been carried out by normal people. Parallels with the Nazi concentration camps during World War II immediately come to mind. It is a sobering lesson to contemplate how the implications of these experimental results might be relevant to a wide range of current human behaviour. It begs the question: are people as responsible as they would like to think of themselves as being? It raises the possibility of conflict between obedience to authority and the idea of individual responsibility.

What society teaches us about the nature of responsibility is two-faced. On the one hand, we learn it is irresponsible to be late for work or to break a law. But, on the other hand, society encourages us to "be happy" and "enjoy" ourselves to excessive degrees – at the expense of ignoring the wider consequences of such self-indulgence, and more or less regardless of what is going wrong in the world. We are taught to be responsible for ourselves and our family, and yet are not urged to help others except in limited ways.

The type of responsibility usually adopted is therefore conditional. It is based on self-interest or mutual self-interest considerations, in keeping with the current general thrust of human nature which views self-orientated behaviour as normal and acceptable. It is a qualified state of responsibility, restricted by the overall strategy of selfishness.

True responsibility is the quality of being genuinely responsive to the world about us. It involves accountability and a willingness to be reliably dependable. There is a preparedness to be trustworthy. To be completely responsive, you need to be fully alive, awake, receptive, sympathetic, and forthcoming. In short, responsibility is the opposite of avoidance.

So there is a conflict between the tendency to avoid and the need for being responsible. This division causes hypocrisy and contradictions, which may or may not be recognised. When the level of expected responsibility increases above an individual's comfort threshold – triggering off avoidance – being responsible might be experienced as a burden. In such instances, you negatively evade or reduce further accountability, or else you constructively learn to be more mature.

Non-selfishness recognises "the-buck-stops-here" variety of responsibility. To achieve this total commitment to life, you need to overcome the wish to shirk or run away from involvement. The limitations of current responsibility is an issue interlinked with the tendency for forgetfulness, making excuses, being complacent, wanting more, and comparing up. These difficulties which make successful change so hard to secure are all part of the same self-defence strategy. Being aware of how it works will at least help loosen the grip of this selfish way of living.

People will sometimes say to someone who is especially sensitive and responsive: "But you can't carry the whole world on your shoulders." These people never go on to explain why this altruism is supposedly impossible. Perhaps such comments are really projections of themselves, reflecting their own psychological weakness and self-justifying arguments for avoidance. Whatever people might like to believe so as to make life "easier", the fact is that we have got to be more genuinely responsible if humankind is to progress and regain a healthy planet. The irresponsible culture of "me, me, me" is not working, as the widespread evidence of suffering clearly demonstrates.

This book started with Sarah's account of how she was raped at the age of 10. Sarah does not think of the stranger who violated her as an evil monster. Instead, she considers he must have been extremely confused, bitter, frustrated,

The burden of responsibility

and psychologically sick. But this explanation is not meant to excuse him, as he must nevertheless be held personally responsible for his hurtful actions. This said, the rapist's family, friends, and acquaintances must also be partly accountable for their part – as sex offenders are not born, but rather in some way conditioned into their bizarre behaviour. On an even wider scale, we must all assume a measure of responsibility because everyone is part of the same society which produces such twisted lives. Unless changed, an intricate web of everyone's pain and avoidance will produce more of the same to varying degrees, with a catalogue of severe incidents occurring at the most unhealthy end of the range. Thus, directly or indirectly, we must all share in the ultimate responsibility.

Responsibility covers our actions and inactions. We have the freedom of choice, whether we choose to use it wisely or not. We each decide what we want and what we actually do, or else we let others decide for us, and so we are responsible – individually and/or collectively – for the consequences. Facing the fact of this fullness of responsibility would be much easier, at least in the long-term, than continually limiting or denying liability. Much effort is wasted through care-less-ly passing the buck. Whereas only a restricted amount of responsibility is generally acknowledged in the self-orientated mind-set, non-selfishness recognises a much greater responsiveness through concern for the whole.

17

Emotional imbalance

Non-selfishness uses the unlimited capacity of *seeing* and *feeling*. It is a totality of interconnected thoughtfulness and caring, resulting in non-selfish action. Using both the head and heart together is all-important. The alternative of normal consciousness is, in contrast, unbalanced. There are degrees of either an irrational emotional approach or an intellectual approach with restricted compassion.

The emotional imbalance of ordinary self-orientated consciousness is fraught with potential difficulties. Two extremes are possible. There might be a strong dependency upon the inner emotions as the dominant motivating force for deciding what to do in life, with a corresponding weakness for rational thought. Or else there might be a strong dependency upon the intellectual approach as one's guiding light, with a neglect of compassionate down-to-earth feeling. More often, people exhibit a muddled compromise; they have developed some acceptance of their intuitive sentiments and some ability for logical reasoning. Whichever dominant tendency is learned or preferred, and to whatever degree, there remains an imbalance. Prejudicial bias to one extreme approach or another will usually result in an intractable divisiveness. It may be near impossible for two people employing these different means of organising their life values and behaviour to have a constructive exchange of views; each might be unable to fully recognise the other's criteria of assessment. The more common mixture of these two approaches is based on selfishness and compromise, which frequently produces a bland acceptance and tendency towards conformity. There is safety in numbers and so probably less motivational drive arises to campaign for radical change.

Emotional imbalance

Someone predominantly acting on their feelings might get carried away by the surge of heart-felt emotion, failing to also consider additional interrelated factors. There is often a predisposition towards single-issue concerns. There is frequently distortion and/or exaggeration within their claims due to the strong emotional focus. Campaigners for greater animal welfare, for example, commonly fall into this category. Emotionally-charged tactics may be used to appeal to other people who are especially sensitive to suffering and thus considered as potential allies. At the opposite extreme, someone predominantly relying on logical reasoning might be denying or blocking off part of their capacity for feeling. Such people can be scornful of others who are unable to argue in a similarly rational manner, perhaps considering themselves to have superior intelligence. An intellectual view of the world allows detachment, perhaps hiding a person's inability to open up and closely empathise with the suffering of others. There might be a more sterile or clinical approach to life. Scientists and lawyers, for example, commonly fall into this category. Mind games, the selective use of words, and an image of elitism may be employed in their pursuit for dominance. Generally, however, most people fall within the mid-range of these two extremes – superficially secure in their normality. They partially agree with both sets of views, albeit usually coming down on one side or another, or perhaps remaining comfortably on the fence between the two. Any sense of commitment is probably limited.

Society accepts the polarity which distances and directs people into the various divisive camps. There is no clear recognition that a capacity exists for much greater thoughtfulness and much greater caring – i.e. that both qualities can and should be fully developed in the same human being. Indeed, we are usually conditioned from an early age to enhance our ability to reason and suppress our ability to care, or vice versa. For example, we are encouraged to become a student of an arts subject or a student of the sciences, but rarely both. (I remember during my own education, at the beginning of the first "A" level year, causing the school timetable to be re-written because I insisted on studying both biology and English literature.) The majority of career jobs do not require you to think and care past a point; in fact, additional thoughtfulness and concern might be actively discouraged if it threatens to rock the boat of stable normality. Society generally exploits the various qualities we have been conditioned into adopting, rather than helping us to develop our full and balanced potential.

A lot of people are therefore categorised by early adulthood. There is probably a self-identification leaning towards being more emotional than rational, or else towards being more rational than emotional. Invariably, whichever way, there is a limitation. Where there is too much dependency upon feeling, illogical thinking and irrational decision-making is likely. An individual overly dependent on feeling for guidance might be incapable of constructing – or responding to – a coherent argument; reason takes second place to raw emotion. Conversely, someone with a well-developed intellect might shy away from their own sensitivity and so will be disadvantaged when a situation calls for emotional maturity and openness.

There are practical consequences of emotional imbalance. Life is viewed in a distorted way. For example, some parents become incapable of a mature response to their young babies. They might start to irrationally believe that a screaming baby is "doing it on purpose to annoy me" – when such sophisticated behaviour is impossible from one so young. Occasionally, this illogical and confused reaction can lead to baby battering. More generally, the job of parenting is a muddled affair with the adults' weaknesses influencing their children's development. Excessive unbalanced feeling can also result in disaster when a person is blinded by love or compassion; the sayings "killing him with kindness" and "sometimes you have to be cruel to be kind" illustrate awareness of this problem. At the other extreme, an ability to intellectually function but avoid a fullness of actual concern can have equally unfortunate consequences. We need only return to my regular example to demonstrate the truth and extent of this. The human race has so far been clever enough to build cars, airplanes, computers, perform complex heart operations, and even travel beyond our planet into space – yet, in 1996, a child in some third world country dies every eight seconds due to diarrhoea, which is just one of many life-threatening illnesses easily treated with low-cost medicine. Why? Because the human race currently limits its caring to pursuing predominantly self-orientated goals. And an assortment of semi-rational excuses, combined with hypocritical complacency, hides this blatantly selfish oversight by normalising the situation. To conclude, an emotional imbalance produces a one-sided bias, with practical consequences, which in some manner helps avoid unwelcome evidence that would be indisputable to an individual with a more psychologically mature approach to life.

Emotional blockages and the inability to properly reason are significant obstacles. These factors, two sides of the same coin, add yet another perspective to the issue of why it is difficult to radically change. The emotional imbalance, either way, restricts genuine openness and true objectivity. Learning is frustrated through this twisted conditioning. There is a strong inclination towards divisiveness and a "them versus us" mentality – or perhaps favouring a mundane conformity for the mid-range individuals – rather than the alternative all-caring, all-inclusive option of non-selfishness.

18

Self-expression

People are self-centred, to a greater or lesser degree, in an obvious or less obvious way. There is therefore the difficulty of self-expression. Some people find it hard to express themselves, sensitive to the fact that they cannot adequately explain what they want to say. Others apparently have no difficulty in communicating or demonstrating what they want, which can be a difficulty of another type.

Feelings of insecurity and self-doubt can be paralysing. Someone can desperately want to change and thereby break out of their suffering, yet feel trapped and incapable of making progress. Such situations seem never-ending – a perpetual nightmare. Heightened anxiety may lead to panic attacks, further adding to the sense of helplessness and inner disability. To some extent, great or minor, you might recognise this feeling of being stuck. Perhaps your experience of it is a general lethargy or complacency, holding you back from changing as much as you could, warily avoiding commitment.

Change involves facing the unknown. Society usually fails to teach people how to do this; indeed, there is more emphasis on maintaining the status quo. You might lack confidence in your ability to succeed at something new, or else be fearful of unfamiliar situations. If you are in a relationship with a partner, perhaps you are worried about how changing could affect this? The worry of anticipation is frequently much greater than the actual reality, but this sensation alone can hold you back. What you need to do is take time out to carefully consider the options. Once you have decided on a choice, evaluate exactly what might be required. If necessary, do some preliminary homework – perhaps by asking questions about the things which are worrying you – before taking the plunge. Think about what

Self-expression

you already know and know how to do, then examine what else you might need to find out and what additional skills you may have to develop. Prepare yourself. This should help reduce much of the anxiety. Then, one step at a time, make a start.

Many people do not, apparently, exhibit a lack of confidence. They appear self-assured and capable. Frequently, however, this outer performance hides another story. What others see might actually be a mask – a front – concealing inner turmoil and some kind of self-doubt. This kind of self-expression is therefore a fragmented part of the whole person. A certain quality has been developed, allowing avoidance or concealment of the painful area. People who constantly clown about, seemingly incapable of any seriousness, are typical examples of this variety of escapism. Showbiz stars often have abundant talent – and a glamourous, wealthy lifestyle – but also a deep insecurity and hidden depression.

Acknowledging this false face can prove difficult. Just as some women will not go out of their house without first putting make-up on, a person might feel dependent upon his or her mental disguise. The limited self-expression becomes a barrier to change, frustrating an all-round potential from unfolding. Overcoming this difficulty first requires knowledge and acceptance of what is happening. Then the habitual dependency must be lessened and finally broken. This can be achieved by setting a series of targets or stages, according to what you feel comfortable in tackling at any particular time. Meanwhile, the hidden part needs to be recognised and given opportunities for expression. The conditioned image of self-identification can thereby be opened to allow renewed personal growth.

A number of people are relatively well balanced. Their capabilities are above average. They are psychologically healthy in normal terms. Such individuals usually get what they want more often than not. They are amongst society's "winners". Life is typically fine. There are no obvious inhibitions of self-expression. Although these apparently lucky people are success stories, they are nevertheless restricted by the image of separateness. Self-orientated behaviour, albeit healthy, still applies.

If you are even moderately successful, why change? Why jeopardise what you have got? This can be an obstacle to further growth. In such instances, a person will probably not be motivated to radically change to benefit themselves. So the motivation has to come from a perception of how others – the whole – would benefit from a shift towards non-selfishness. The incentive must be altruistic, rather than self-seeking. This process of opening up will need to involve a sensitive awareness of the suffering of others, combined with an understanding that self-orientated behaviour is the fundamental cause of most problems. And the individual must be willing to learn, despite prior achievements and success. There has to be a starting anew, with a fresh attitude. Otherwise, existing self-expression will cultivate complacency and hinder progress.

Compliance with traditional values has exerted considerable constraint on individual behaviour. In recent times, this cultural influence has been relaxed. There is less respect for authority and conformity. Individualism is increasingly gaining the upper hand. Customary moral restrictions and social taboos are losing their power of deterrence. Self-expression is becoming all-important. In many ways, this shift of behaviour is to be welcomed. It is a movement towards liberation from unnecessary guilt and numerous "supposed-to-be" conventions. There are more opportunities and a greater freedom of choice for individual expression. Assertiveness is actively encouraged by self-help workshops to enhance people's capacity for saying what they want. The term "empowerment" has received widespread acclaim.

Acknowledging that there are clear benefits to this increasing individualism, it then has to be said that a potential difficulty is also arising. What is "empowerment" actually empowering? In short, selfishness is being strengthened. Self-orientated behaviour is being improved.

Self-expression

People are learning to demand their rights and to better express their individualism. This does not necessarily have anything directly to do with non-selfishness. Moreover, it may harden the nut that needs to be cracked.

It is ironic that the so-called "new age" movement has enthusiastically embraced this drive for "empowerment". Having failed to properly grasp what is involved in making the shift to a genuinely enlightened consciousness, the various counsellors and personal development teachers have quickly latched on to this lesser goal. Superficial results are easy to achieve and the self-indulgent "feel good" factor is always available to be exploited. People are eager to feel better about themselves, yet still neglect to significantly broaden their caring for others. A self-obsessed "new age" industry has found a good way to liberate the gullible and the confused of their emotional burdens, as well as their money. The "sharing" of workshops seems to me like a licence to wallow in self-pity and/or become more self-confident. It has little to do with spirituality. Interestingly, this popular application of psychology is perhaps being most welcomed in the fields of business and high-finance sport. The potential of strengthening individual competitiveness for selfish gain has seen an eruption of personal growth gurus. "Let's get rich without feeling guilty about it!" "Greater and better self-satisfaction!" "Learn how to achieve the dreams of your desire!" "Win! Win! Win!" Clearer self-expression is definitely needed, but will it alone really make the world a better place? Or is this means of mental manipulation being exploited, like material resources, for selfish gain?

19

Get over it!

Self-obsession takes many forms. You feel sorry for yourself or you self-indulge. It may be expressed in a mental, physical, or even pseudo-spiritual way. There is an imbalance caused by too much attachment to "me, me, me" considerations. This difficulty is in direct conflict with the way of non-selfishness. You need to get over it!

A lot of people bask in self-indulgence. They glorify their personal achievements and delight in self-orientated success, at the expense of caring for everyone and everything. Or, if their own life is mundane, people might live through the fantasy images of others more successful than themselves – such as showbiz stars or sporting heroes. Money is frequently worshipped as the new god, as money is thought of by many as being able to buy happiness (or at least to help get most of what you want).

Food is a common object of desire which produces immediate gratification. Millions get fat as a result, then worry about dieting – apparently oblivious of the wider world in which millions of others continue to suffer from malnutrition or starvation. Some honestly admit their problem and seek help. But many of those who over-eat and then attempt to diet, but time after time fail, are increasingly claiming that they now actually enjoy being fat – conveniently denying the fact that obesity is a serious threat to personal health and a drain on their country's medical services. This makes the vicious circle even more difficult to break. In almost every case, food problems are just the outer indication of some inner dilemma. This self-indulgence syndrome keeps sufferers from having to confront and deal with their deeper problems. Why bother yourself with serious self-examination, or going to a shrink, when the fridge door offers instant salvation? Fat people

Get over it!

are laughed at as objects of ridicule and this is wrong. They are still individuals with real feelings. Their inner problems are merely shown outwardly, physically, whereas other people are more easily able to hide their particular inadequacies through self-indulging in different ways. Any type of prejudice is unhelpful; but when fat people blame the small-mindedness of others for their own suffering, this causes an additional problem, usefully distracting attention away from the primary difficulties.

The "losers" in society often wallow in their self-pity. Convinced that they will not be successful by their own merit, these individuals then learn to make a career out of their failure. They exploit the misfortune, making the most of their losing streak. Such people learn to like being unhappy, finding that they get attention and an odd sort of pleasure from their misery. If a hypochondriac is someone who has an imaginary anxiety about their health, a person who indulgently wallows in self-pity might be called a happy-chondriac.

Some individuals discover that the victim mentality gets sympathy and so they develop into emotional vampires, draining people of their compassion. Others turn their bad luck into an opportunity to get what they want, by finding someone other than themselves to blame. Denying personal responsibility for their own actions, they search for a reason to pin the fault on another. This might result in financial compensation, perhaps after being encouraged by lawyers to instigate legal proceedings. Never mind the overall consequences, such as off-duty doctors and nurses being scared to help a collapsed person on the street in case they end up being sued. Empowering selfishness is like opening up Pandora's box.

Bitterness and resentment can become self-consuming. Feeling sorry for yourself can delude you into thinking that the world owes you a favour. Seeing what others have got breeds discontentment. You may start believing that you also deserve to live like a king, but without having to first work for it. This is how thieves usually justify their excessively selfish actions. Others do similar things in a legal manner. Some over-spend, seeking credit above their means to repay, ending up in debt. Some learn to exploit the social security system and make a permanent living through claiming every entitlement originally intended to help the genuinely disadvantaged at a time of need. More of the "take, take, take" mentality.

Selfishness involves lazy-mindedness and limited concern. An emotional imbalance and a degree of irrationality is accepted as normal. In turn, this may lead to a tendency for moaning, groaning, and bitching. This is a likely consequence when there is self-preoccupation and an avoidance of personal responsibility. Moaning, groaning, and bitching gives you something to do when it is hard to accept the full reality. You displace your feelings of discomfort. Rather than seeking a way forward, off-loading on to someone or something else provides an easy – if short-term – method of releasing stress and frustration. It is similar to a young child throwing a tantrum when he/she fails to get what he/she wants. An immature strategy, but one which nevertheless usually gets noticed. Bitching at someone else diverts the nature of attention. You blow someone else's candle out so as to make your own burn brighter.

Political correctness has provided a comfortable means of hiding behind words. Use of clever or "safe" language can mask practical ineptitude. It conveniently gets a variety of people off the hook, side-stepping real accountability. Plain speaking is increasingly regarded as being potentially offensive – a trend which makes it more difficult to expose what is wrong in society. Political correctness is an inadequate superficial answer to a deep-seated problem. Wallpapering over the cracks may look good to begin with, but it is an unreliable means of repair; the inevitable is merely delayed. Shit is still shit, whatever name you use. And it is not going to go away unless recognised as shit, then cleared up.

The inclination towards self-pity and self-indulgence adds to the general proneness for complacency. It is usually a sign of poor self-discipline. Various techniques have been developed by the spiritual traditions to counteract this problem, usually involving a trend towards austerity. Military training has also recognised this need to overcome self-pity and self-indulgence, employing a similar psychological approach to break the egotistical wallowing. Greater reliability can be predicted when there are fewer selfish distractions – leaving someone with a more alert, objective awareness.

20

The fear of letting go

The majority of people are afraid to let go. They are fearful of taking chances, unwilling to put their existing security at risk. The need for safety and self-defence dominates. This reluctance to make major changes can be readily observed in many people within the range of ordinary behaviour. People often wish to change, but they usually look for a guarantee to go with it.

Personal growth is generally conditional. The question "Do I feel safe enough to change?" is knowingly or intuitively considered as an initial factor. If the answer is affirmative, a step forward might be possible. It is a matter of inner security and self-confidence. Other self-interest issues are likewise examined. Will I benefit? What do I stand to gain? How will any resulting alterations affect my wider lifestyle? Therefore, deliberate personal growth invariably occurs only when the self-orientated advantages are attractive and threats to self-security are perceived as minimal or nil. This criteria is biased towards maintaining selfishness. Any change is limited. Where growth is identified with spirituality or the development of consciousness, concepts of wholeness and interconnected belonging are perverted into a selfish version of this potential.

As a preliminary condition, a state of reasonable psychological health and inner security is helpful prior to attempting a fundamental shift of consciousness. The alternatives of selfishness and non-selfishness can thus be examined and assessed in a mature, caring, and rational way before any decision is made. Specific emotional disorders or blatant instabilities particular to an individual need to be dealt with first if they threaten a generally balanced approach. If not, such neuroses may hinder the

The fear of letting go

complete shift to non-selfishness, perhaps producing a distorted interpretation reflecting the person's psychological disorder.

The fear of letting go all self-attachments is understandable. Letting go is contrary to the normally accepted strategy of putting personal safety and desire first. To an individual newly considering the non-selfish option, the future may seem like an abyss. He or she usually cannot imagine a pure non-selfish way of life. It undermines the conventional identifications that people ordinarily relate to – challenging the things which make up their identity. Scared to jump into the bottomless depth of non-selfishness, the immature aspirant usually retreats back from the edge and searches for what appears to be a safer option.

A parallel is easy to see with many meat-eaters when the subject of a vegetarian diet is discussed. A permanent diet without meat, fowl, or fish is often incomprehensible to the non-vegetarian; they cannot imagine it as a realistic, preferable, and tasty option. All they see is deprivation and the giving up of something they like. "What? No meat?!" Their personal desires are rigidly held as the primary concern, neglectful of the unnecessary suffering and killing involved. To them, meat is synonymous with eating. Turkey and Christmas dinner are perceived as going together.

It can be expected that a fear of letting go will arise at some point. An awkward sensitivity to this dilemma is part of the awakening process as the need for a new decision begins to be understood. It should not be denied. Neither is it a sign of weakness, unless unnecessarily prolonged through indecisive pondering. Facing this fear of the unknown must be done if selfishness is to be outgrown. Egotistical safety and defence are currently integral parts of the self-orientated option. They are, however, irrelevant to the non-selfish alternative. This discrepancy or divergence must be recognised and accepted. Letting go of selfish desires should be seen as an attractive choice, basic to non-selfishness – in a similar way that giving up meat is fundamental to becoming a vegetarian.

Actions Speak Louder Than Words

The fear of letting go can be crippling and may prevent or limit personal growth. This difficulty is especially heightened in the choice between selfishness and non-selfishness, as the dilemma is bluntly exposed. Fear can be understood in this instance, however, as nothing more than fear itself. It is self-created, self-perpetuating, and irrational. It results from the image of separateness, which has built up the strategy of "me, me, me". Whereas a fear of letting go might be useful for preserving egotistical safety and defence, it has no value with regards to the option of non-selfishness. Careful consideration of this matter in light of the above comments should ease any tension and help assist the way forward.

21

Awareness is not the same as achievement

Armchair philosophers can have great awareness. I used to know such a person many years ago who had really thought deeply about the meaning of life. A genuinely considerate person, sensitive and caring, as well as widely read and thoughtful. But he liked sitting on his couch too much. He could give you an answer to most points, except when I occasionally reminded him of a local instance of two bored young lads who had hammered several six-inch nails into the back of a donkey. This acute reminder of harsh reality always disturbed his inner contentment. I guess he knew that his armchair philosophy seemed an inadequate response.

Insight is of limited usefulness if not applied. Knowledge is knowing some factual information. Wisdom is knowing what to do with this knowledge. Hypocrisy occurs when you know or believe one thing, yet do something different due to avoidance or complacency. Actions speak louder than words.

Increased awareness can provide an illusion of change. At the moment of realisation, a fresh perception is noticeable. The new awareness may fade or remain. If it stays, you might have advanced your level of understanding, but nevertheless could still be acting in the old habitual patterns as before. Awareness is not the same as achievement. There is the danger of hypocrisy. There can be a gap between what you think and feel, and what you actually do in outer practice. This problem of not putting fully into action what you believe or would like to do is a widespread human trait. Awareness gives you a comfortable couch or armchair – a safe inner world of imagination – to explore and act out your boldest ideas. It might have a subjective meaning to you, but it remains of little or no use to the objective reality of everyday life unless translated into action. Wonderful thoughts may exist, but they do not alone help to stop or prevent actual suffering.

Awareness is to do with the mind. It is the growth of an individual's inner experience. As important as this inward psychological expansion is, we must always realise that awareness might be just another form of self-preoccupation. We therefore need to assess the results of any new insight. This is the essential anti-hypocrisy test: actions speak louder than words. We must look for both awareness and the application of awareness; together, these complementary factors will indicate the depth or true worth of insight.

I cannot emphasise enough that awareness is only awareness, unless applied through practical endeavours. A corresponding change of activity should always follow any heightened perception. Awareness in isolation is unbalanced and effectively self-indulgent. Inner development must be matched with outer development.

A person's awareness is usually in itself unbalanced. As discussed in Chapter 17, there is greater prominence of either the rational, conceptual, understanding side or of the heart-felt empathy and caring aspect. When one of these two elements is incomplete, the potential for self-deception exists. If awareness is predominantly intellectual, there is often a degree of sterility or cold detachment from the real suffering of others. If, on the other hand, an emotionally biased perception prevails, there might be a lack of precise thinking and/or broad-mindedness. When there is sufficient insight of an equally proportionate nature, the dangers of delusion and duplicity have no place. The two sides of awareness must be balanced, and awareness needs to be translated into appropriate action.

The purpose of awareness is to facilitate interaction with life. Consciousness allows being. A mature awareness will be able to fully experience and deal with reality. An immature awareness will partly avoid reality, caused through a lack of understanding and motivated by wanting to minimise the corresponding emotional turmoil. People's responses to particular situations can therefore usually be predicted. For example, a problem occurs and is identified. The immature response might be to shy away and keep quiet, or else to scornfully criticise. Either reaction is unhelpful, excluding, and self-orientated. The mature response would be to offer constructive criticism and perhaps additional help, with the insight that the problem could be overcome and future repetitions prevented. This reaction is solution-orientated and demonstrates a willing involvement.

A limited amount of knowledge and awareness can be a trap to further progress. It can result in aloof arrogance and a conceited image of self-importance. It can produce a torrent of verbal diarrhoea. What you know becomes a consuming focus and you forget what you still need to learn. Certain doors remain closed. Those who really know realise the need to share and interconnect. There is no standoffish distancing from others. They lead by the practical example of action, as well as urging others towards increased participation with life through the use of words. A person trapped by what he or she knows will demonstrate a weakness of outer involvement; if capable in some area, there will be avoidance of other valid concerns.

22

The blind leading the blind

A limited amount of knowledge and awareness can be addictive. You can easily become dependent upon what you know, or think you know, blind to other considerations. Awareness can thus feed the ego or self-centred individual. This danger equally applies to awareness of spirituality or higher consciousness matters, as in other walks of life. False teachers thereby emerge, full of what they think they know, perhaps largely neglectful of what they do not know and still need to learn. A situation arises of the blind leading the blind.

Reliance on knowledge and ability is different from a reliance based on belief. Knowledge and ability can be objectively tested and replicated, regardless of dogma. Belief, however, relies on subjective faith. A fullness of rational explanation is suspended or considered impossible. It might be of limited use as an initial aid for searching, but belief should never become a permanent replacement for knowledge and ability. Unfortunately, belief often encourages complacency, lazy-mindedness, and long-term dependency. It perpetuates the illusion of searching, actually turning it into following, frustrating advanced progress. Security is preferred to the possibility of fully finding. The comfort of group companionship is chosen over the more lonely path of exploration. Belief is the easier option to knowledge and ability. It is the way of sheep.

Disbelief is the other side of belief. It is belief in reverse. Again, it provides a convenient alternative to the more demanding criteria of knowledge and ability. Both disbelief and belief provide the means for bitching and bickering. They are mental barriers to unity, defining lines of division and disagreement, encouraging emotional protection. You are pushed into a closed "for" or "against" judgement,

The blind leading the blind

taking sides. Openness to not knowing – and therefore the possibility of finding – is forfeited.

Belief offers a psychological crutch and the opportunity to join an entertainment club. It is different from a wish for straightforward education. Various "isms" have thus emerged as popular movements. Conventional religions and their factional sects. Cults. The so-called "new age" mixture of philosophies, therapies, and incredulous mumbo-jumbo. A belief in materialism and the god of money.

Traditional/institutional beliefs are an unreliable source of knowledge. The teachings are likely to be contaminated with irrelevant additions, possibly covering up important omissions, and thus misrepresented to some extent. Additional problems of misinterpretation and genuine differences of meaning due to translation will probably be encountered. The situation is not helped by the fact that few individuals have experienced a constant and full enlightenment. Generally, they wrote down nothing in their own words. In recent times, a number of books have been published containing the teachings of several contemporary gurus of doubtful authenticity; references to the need for non-selfish action seem to be noticeably absent, suggesting that caution might be wise. Whereas the large amount of historical and modern literature contains a great deal of collective wisdom and truisms, it is an uphill struggle for the serious student to sort out the genuine from the dubious, let alone the essential from the non-essential. Precise guidelines are cluttered. Even more relevant and telling is the lack of human beings demonstrating pure non-selfishness, obvious by their absence. Therefore, the scarcity of access to living enlightened individuals and their reliable knowledge gained through direct experience has proved to be a major obstacle to learning.

This shortage of pioneers who have achieved a total breakthrough of consciousness – and the failure of these occasional trailblazers to assist others to the same awareness – has resulted in the mushrooming of a secondary level of spiritual teachers with a less than complete understanding.

These usually knowledgeable and/or wise individuals have often been well-intentioned, although not always, but their guidance has been flawed. Often, they have totally missed some of the essential points. Further down the ladder of awareness, many others are exploiting the widespread general searching for that "something more" in ways that frequently ignore logical reasoning and the daily reality of what is happening in the world. In the absence of clear non-hypocritical instruction and leadership by example, people are left to wander without a precise map or route. In this uncharted wilderness, thieves and unscrupulous guides abound, ready to prey on the naive traveller.

The mechanisms of enlightenment or non-selfish consciousness combine together as precisely as the components in a television set. If a television is missing a single component, it will not work properly. And all the electrical parts need to be in the correct sequence. The television set then needs to be switched on and tuned. It is an exact exercise, without which there will be no functioning – or, at best, only a distorted blur of sound and vision. Faith or belief is no substitute for an electrician's technical know-how. The same is true of non-selfishness.

With billions of people walking around in normal or ordinary consciousness, presumptions and beliefs are too easily accepted and so continue. The religious authorities encourage faith, rather than open-mindedness; they want to convert. The huge amount of belief and mumbo-jumbo thrives because it is not being seriously challenged by those seeking additional meaning to life. There is indulgence and bland acceptance, whereas a disciplined clarity of mind is needed. Who is going to question and re-question the fundamental issue of self-orientated behaviour, when people are themselves still more or less operating from the same limited perspective? Those in positions of institutional or sectarian group power are hardly likely to be the first to hold up their hands and admit that they do not have all the answers. Few are honest enough to declare their hypocrisy. So the blind will continue to lead the blind in the game of seek and follow.

23

Heading for chaos?

Most animals interact with the world about them as a result of their instinctive biological conditioning, with some modification through learned experience. In contrast, human behaviour exhibits a much greater reliance on learning from the society of which the individual is a part. Humans make culture, but are also made by culture. Our lifestyles are shaped by the traditions into which we are born and live. Nowadays, the fast pace of technological advancement is producing increased opportunities. Old customs are breaking down, with greater individual freedom arising. But there are also new problems. What do these changes mean? Will the future make the shift towards non-selfishness easier or more difficult? What do current trends throughout the world suggest?

We live in a global economy where finance is international in scope. Businesses are becoming more mobile. They can buy, manufacture, and sell anywhere in the world according to the best means to make a profit. Governments of emerging industrialised countries are encouraging foreign companies to invest, offering cheaper labour and other incentives. Technology is widely available – for those who can afford it. All this competitive activity of mass production and consumerism has been generated by the "I want more" mentality. It is a self-perpetuating marketplace.

Television in particular has informed the poor about how the rich live – heightening expectations and discontentment. Satellite technology has recently made the reception of television programmes accessible to even the remotest areas of our planet. It is now possible to see occasional satellite dishes in the mountain communities of Nepal where roads have yet to penetrate. Together with similar modern influences from other sources, long-established traditional values and lifestyles are being rejected by the informed younger generations, who are tempted by the glamour and glitter on offer. This rapid change is more like a hurried breakdown, rather than the gradual transition associated with previous progress. Lured by short-term gratification, people are jumping without considering the long-term implications. Money has become the new god – the presumed answer to all their problems.

Future trends are uncertain. There will be less apparent stability. Exploitative materialism looks set to continue, unless the environmental movement quickly matures and deepens its wider message to every family of the world. With traditional values being weakened, individualism is growing. People are learning the lessons of empowerment, making them less restrained and better at getting what they want. Selfishness is being unleashed. But employment opportunities are changing. There is less job security than known by previous generations. Businesses are relocating. Other countries are now energetically competing for a share of the world market. Assumed standards of lifestyle will become threatened. The gap between the "have's" and the "have not's" will increase further, with the mid-range "have's" often struggling to hang on to their security. In many cases, anxiety and stress will stifle the possibility of letting go and choosing anew. Isolationism and a fortress mentality will grow. Many individuals will seek the security of factional groups to help them fight for a slice of the pie. Politicians will be less and less able to deliver their election promises to the people. Order will frequently break down, with localised chaotic outbursts of frustration and resentment. Indeed, this future prediction is already starting to happen.

The wider world is very different to what most people in the richer countries see outside their windows. Large migrations of people are beginning to occur, desperate for the chance of sharing the advertised dream of wealth and all it promises to bring. Will economic refugees become the new enemy? When people are marginalised, you get a return to tribalism. Criminals, youth gangs, drug addicts, religious fanatics, militant ethnic groups, and other minorities – even whole countries – will escalate their activities in response to the feeling of being neglected. The consequence of one set of people exploiting another sooner or later produces a backlash effect, which in turn continues the disharmony. The "we-no-longer-need-you" attitude breeds bitterness. Disenchanted groups then start demanding something for nothing. The mediocre majority quickly blame these so-called troublemakers, partly with good reason, but failing to acknowledge or understand the underlying cause of the problems. Again, the early signs of this possible future trend are already apparent for those willing to take notice.

With more and more people disinhibited from traditional constraints, we should expect excesses in conventional behaviour. Sometimes this liberation will produce abnormal reactions. Anyone who is reluctant to adapt to this fast changing society will perceive security as a more precious commodity than at present, no longer able to be taken for granted. The culture of selfishness will intensify. Scarcity of certain resources, over-population, crime, tribalism, and disease are ravaging the structure of social cohesiveness. Will this tighten the grip of the self-orientated mind-set, or point towards the need for a non-selfish alternative?

The choice is up to us all. We urgently have to openly examine what is happening and why. The possibility of needing to fundamentally shift direction must be considered in detail. We should guard against the temptation to superficially wallpaper over the cracks, or blame any particular section of society. Perhaps there is no easy time to let go and face the unknown? Hoping for that mythical right moment or wishing for the helpful hand of a fairy godmother is just putting off the inevitable. So why wait for further unnecessary suffering to teach us that we must develop a better way of living together? We have to recognise that every one of us has an individual choice. We can each help to chose the future, beginning now. We talk about global awareness, but it must be equally matched with global responsibility.

24

An "impossible dream"?

No human being would ever be able to run a mile in under four minutes – that's what all the experts said. But, on 6th May 1954, Roger Bannister broke the "impossible" four-minute mile. John Landy, an Australian, had previously failed to get within two seconds of going under the four-minute target, despite a number of serious attempts. He became doubtful if anyone would run fast enough in the next ten years. Yet just 46 days after Roger Bannister's famous success, John Landy ran even faster to gain a new world record. Several dozen other runners also ran quicker than four minutes during the first year after Roger Bannister had proved that it was possible to break the barrier. Many more did so again the following year. Derek Ibbotson made history with an even faster time in July 1957. Herb Elliot ran faster still in August 1958. Others have since continued to lower the world record.

What occurred in the 1950s – a period before sophisticated sports training – was initially a matter of determined imagination. Roger Bannister dared to challenge the prevailing belief that a sub-four-minute mile was impossible. Together with a couple of others, he analysed how to achieve the dream. Once the record was broken, the flood gates opened. Such fast times became actually possible. The psychological barrier vanished, other than personal self-confidence considerations. As more people ran under four minutes, it became more and more achievable. People's perception had changed. All of the world record holders mentioned above recognise this critical psychological factor.

I am sure that this "Roger Bannister effect" will be seen in the future to have applied to the breakthrough of non-selfish consciousness. Enlightenment, in the complete sense, has apparently been an extremely rare historical event. We pioneers have been occasional freaks of nature. The hard evidence suggests that we have so far failed to assist the duplication of this "new" consciousness in others as an achievable and constant potential. It has remained a dream, an ideal, and a subject of belief in the minds of those interested. It has generally been regarded as a godlike state. Although radically different from the range of present behaviour, it is nevertheless a human potential and available to all. Sometimes, others have underestimated what is involved. We need to demonstrate that non-selfishness is a real alternative which can be achieved by anyone willing to make the shift. We must show the achievability of this potential. A multiple example is required. One person is not enough.

A high-quality example of at least several dozen individuals might be enough to kick-start the process necessary to eventually achieve a breakthrough of consciousness for the whole human race. Although exact knowledge is essential to make the shift, the majority of people also need to be convinced that it is achievable and worthwhile. At present, choices (including spirituality) are only visible in the ordinary self-orientated range. The non-selfish alternative is either unknown or unclear. This is a major difficulty frustrating change. We have to make the alternative real and available, here and now. Although many have attempted to gain enlightenment, precise instructions have usually been lacking as previously discussed. Belief, mumbo-jumbo, and irrelevant philosophy hinder progress. The issue has to be de-mystified.

Excellence and integrity should characterise this multiple example. Individuals must be independently-minded, yet freely willing to work together. They each need to demonstrate a balanced competence. The ability to think more, care more, and do more must be developed in a combined manner. Anything less than an 80% shift – where 0% is normal consciousness and 100% is complete non-selfishness – would be unsuitable as part of this suggested example. Whereas it does not have to be perfect, a high degree of contrast is required to signify the non-selfish alternative. It is not enough just to be able to understand more, or to have greater concern, or to demonstrate apparent unselfishness in action; all three elements are part of an integrated whole.

If several dozen individuals working together were able to make such a significant shift, a clear indication could then be presented to others as evidence of a worthwhile initiative. The perception of achievability for all would increase – the possibility of a non-selfish lifestyle no longer a vague potential or an occasional oddity. Additional serious participants would gradually be willing to join in, allowing further kick-start examples. The "Roger Bannister effect" should become noticeable. Maintaining excellence and integrity would be vitally important; quality in preference to quantity. Later, as wider public interest becomes aroused, a general education programme would be crucial to explain the concept and benefits of non-selfishness. A growing movement should guard against suggestions of elitism or any threatening signs of "us versus them". It is an educational process, taught by example, with no-hypocrisy as its standard of measurement.

The task, on an individual level, is a major undertaking. Serious commitment is required to see it through to fruition. But the same is true of becoming a doctor. The global scale of bringing about a radical shift towards non-selfish perception and values is an even bigger, almost impossible task. But it can be done. The blockage to making a start, apart from the lack of a clear conception of the options, involves the question of achievability. Can it be done? Will it be a waste of time and effort? It necessitates a long-term view and initial courage. A prospective candidate might consider this ancient Tibetan saying:

It is better to have lived as a tiger for a single day, than as a sheep for a thousand years.

SECTION FOUR: NON-SELFISHNESS

25

Approaching the start-line

Non-selfishness is a radically different alternative to normal or ordinary consciousness. It is not the same as what is currently perceived to be unselfish or "good" behaviour. The latter occurs at the healthier end of a range of conventional behaviour, with obviously selfish or "bad" behaviour at the less healthy end of the same range. Non-selfishness has no basis in this self-orientated range of human activity. It is completely different.

It is important to stress this point so as to avoid possible misunderstanding. I hope the following analogy will help further clarify what I am trying to convey. There is a clear, unambiguous distinction between a smoker and a non-smoker. Someone who smokes could be anywhere along a range of smoking activity. He or she might smoke 60 cigarettes per day and be at the "heavy smoker" end of the range. Or an individual may only smoke one or two cigarettes occasionally, perhaps as more of a social habit, and so be at the opposite end of the range. But both must be classified as smokers, distinctly different from non-smokers. Similarly, there is a connection between so-called "bad" or obviously selfish behaviour and so-called "good" or apparently unselfish behaviour. Not even the apparently unselfish end of this self-orientated spectrum is the same as non-selfishness, although there might be a number of similarities.

The range of normal or ordinary consciousness is characterised or linked by a fundamental image of separateness. This image of separateness results in a greater emphasis on "me", "my", or "us" than on "them", thereby causing a division or duality. Different standards apply, favouring "me", "my", or "us" above and before "them". These dual standards might be obvious or subtle, according to someone's degree of functioning along the range of self-orientated behaviour. By contrast, non-selfishness is free of all selfishness. Individuality remains, but the roots of being are in oneness, wholeness, or interconnectedness. This is emphatically not a matter of belief, ideas, or words; rather, it is an achievable coherent psychology demonstrated through outer action.

The non-selfish option can be temporarily glimpsed to different degrees of clarity, occasionally as a total or full exposure. However, normal self-orientated consciousness quickly returns, albeit perhaps profoundly challenged. True non-selfishness only begins when selfishness has been completely dissolved as an on-going and constant experience.

Non-selfishness is a tremendous potential waiting to be developed. It seems to exist already in people as something which is buried, neglected, misunderstood, denied, or suppressed. When it is searched for and attempts made to unfold it, the potential appears to be fragile and easily distorted. It is probably something deep within our nature at a pre-conditioned, pre-moral, and pre-cultural level.

Human beings are, of course, extremely complex in their psychology and behaviour. Everyone is in some way unique, having developed according to a different combination of outer experiences and inner responses. But the active foundation of human conduct seems to be identical in billions of people: the selfish factor of "me" and "my" is more or less dominant. Kindness and concern for others is generally a secondary consideration, able to be expressed when the "me" is not going to lose out or get in the way. It is this self-orientated element – the image of separateness – which limits and frustrates human potential. This is the root of the problem. This is the linchpin on which

Approaching the start-line

everything is dependent. A completely different foundation or starting-point is therefore required. The self-orientated factor is the crucial part which needs to be challenged and replaced. Genuine non-selfish interconnectedness is the basic alternative. Non-selfishness offers a different choice to that of the usual selfish conditioning. It provides the opportunity for profound and radical change, as opposed to mere adaptations which are essentially variations of the same thing. The diagram used in Chapter 5 may again help to illustrate what I am trying to explain:

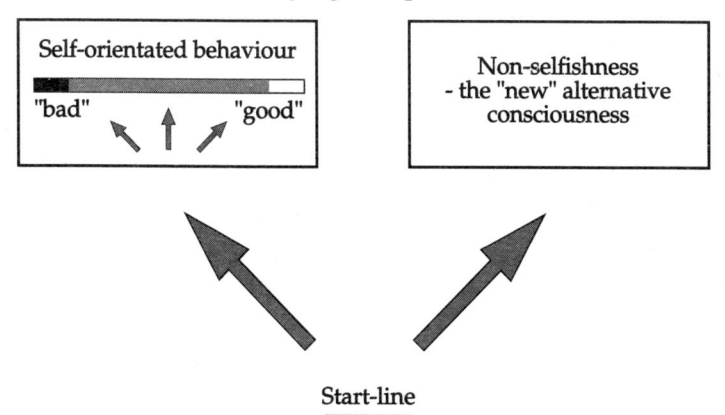

```
┌─────────────────────────────┐   ┌─────────────────────────────┐
│ Self-orientated behaviour   │   │    Non-selfishness          │
│ ▆▆▆▆▆▆▆▆▆▆▁▁▁▁▁▁            │   │  - the "new" alternative    │
│ "bad"   ↖ ↑ ↗  "good"       │   │      consciousness          │
└─────────────────────────────┘   └─────────────────────────────┘

              ↖                         ↗

                       Start-line
                       ─────────
```

The shift from selfishness to non-selfishness is not a continuum. It is not a matter of personal growth as conventionally understood, which will only produce a change along the self-orientated range towards "good" or more healthy selfish behaviour. A complete and fresh assessment of the whole situation has to be made. You need to stand back – a long way back – so as to be able to view and consider the two options: selfishness or non-selfishness? This standing back and assessing the situation is more fundamental than normally realised. It may appear similar to the aspirant's prior attempts at choosing "alternatives", but in reality these former "choices" were actually just opportunities within the same range. The two basic alternatives are clearly distinct – in a similar way to the earlier example of being a smoker or non-smoker – and the initial awareness of this might seem staggering. The non-selfish choice is a path involving a fundamentally different strategy. It calls for a break with selfish considerations. Doing it on an individual level is hard enough; global change will require even greater effort. It is an option which, from the current viewpoint, is an almost impossible task. Nevertheless, this is the choice facing a prospective pioneer.

Most interested people have never properly begun to shift from selfishness to non-selfishness. They have simply not gone back far enough to the beginning. They fail to realise the distinctive options, or else settle for the easier path of personal growth within the self-orientated range. They may become "good". Much pseudo-spiritual activity has thus occurred, which is different from – although, at times, similar to – the real thing. Misunderstandings have arisen from an incomplete perspective and/or due to an avoidance of the selfish core. Though often well-intentioned, people's efforts to gain enlightenment – complete freedom from selfish limitations – have been doomed to fail.

Non-selfishness should not be mistaken as being selfless. Individuality is not given up nor annihilated. You are part of the whole and realise this as such. Although attention is shifted from all selfish desire to concerns of the whole, recognition of genuine individual needs and expression remains. You do not become a doormat. Only the selfish considerations are dumped. It is the grossly distorted self-orientated perspectives – emerging from the conditioned image of separateness – which require challenging and re-assessment. Whereas speculation about such a drastic change may seem to indicate the end of individuality – oblivion of the self – this is just because most people's identity is made up of selfish factors; there is identification with what "I want" and the "how I think I am" labelling. Sweep away all such conditioning and a unique non-selfish individuality survives within an interconnected context.

Approaching the start-line

Approaching the start-line is all-important. You need to know where it is or what it is. You need a clear appreciation of the two different alternatives: selfishness or non-selfishness? You need to evaluate the benefits and disadvantages of self-orientated behaviour. These findings then need to be assessed according to the non-selfish alternative. Which option is better? Are the differences – any potential benefits for the individual and/or the whole offered by non-selfishness – worth the effort of changing? (This awareness will provide the necessary motivation, especially when the evaluation takes into account real instances of suffering.) You then need a conceptual understanding of what has to be changed, what difficulties might threaten to impede any efforts to change, and what exactly you have to do to successfully make the shift. (The formula for change is outlined in the next chapter.) Then, with this preliminary appraisal completed, you are ready to make the crucial first step.

The start-line is a position from which you can make a fundamental decision. The choice is simple: selfishness or non-selfishness? It is a decision which calls for honesty, level-headedness, caring, courage, and personal responsibility. Whichever option you select, this will be your chosen route and destination. Having been conditioned into the self-orientated mind-set, this is an opportunity for you to play a part in determining the future from a position of free will selection. Your decision fixes the direction of your first step and subsequent steps – unless you reverse the decision or weaken your resolve. The choice initially establishes your commitment to one option or the other. If selfishness is selected, you return to the familiar where habit takes over. If non-selfishness is selected, you face a pioneering journey. Your decision will be tested and re-tested, as a struggle against habitual reactions and the on-going conditioning of society. Are you really prepared to change – to unlearn and re-learn – and to give the process consistent priority? You will need a route map to follow, giving you the necessary directions and knowledge of what is involved, without which you would probably wander haphazardly.

Standing at the start-line, seeing both options before you, the decision process might seem to be an easy matter of selecting non-selfishness. Experience of present realities of everyday life should theoretically make your choice a foregone conclusion. Non-selfishness is by far the better alternative, albeit as yet largely untried by the human race. But the power of conditioning must not be underestimated. There are the safety factors to hold you back; self-defence strategies have been acquired through previous painful experience. A lack of confidence in your abilities might also hinder you. There is some security in the conventional known, and risk in the unknown. "Better the devil you know....." etc. And then there are your selfish wants and ambitions, together with your existing self-orientated lifestyle. Forgetfulness, excuses, and complacency will perhaps further jeopardise any inclination to change. So, in actual practice, most people find the choice difficult; many shy away from attempting the shift to non-selfishness. Selfish factors might dominate, or the dilemma could be resolved by indecision. Often someone may hope/believe that spiritual progress or an expansion of human potential will occur some other (unspecified) way. It is important to be aware of all these various factors as part of your preparation prior to the decision making.

Millions of people have beliefs and philosophies with the unifying theme of love and understanding as a central issue. Yet so often these beliefs and ideas remain as little more than good intentions and comforting crutches. A gap is generally noticeable between a person's thinking and feeling and his or her outer actions. This hypocrisy factor will be examined in more detail in Chapter 27, but it is relevant here in discussing how to approach the start-line. Integrity is required. Greater seriousness is needed. Suffering is real and widespread. As most suffering is caused by selfish behaviour, it will surely continue, in one form or another, until the root cause is engaged and

Approaching the start-line

transformed. A number of pioneers are essential to demonstrate that the journey to non-selfishness is both achievable by anyone and beneficial to all. Personal sacrifices are necessary and the shifting of consciousness may not always be smooth, but the eventual results are more than worthwhile. (No Olympic champion ever succeeded without consistent, serious training, nor regretted the years of effort after reaching that peak of achievement.) When approaching the start-line and making your decision – selfishness or non-selfishness? – please remember that this is not some intellectual exercise or game. If your inclinations are towards love and understanding, combined with practicality, this is a crucial opportunity for greater maturity. This is *your* chance to make a real difference.

26

The formula for change

He who knows does not speak.
He who speaks does not know.
                Lao Tsu

The "new" non-selfish strategy is very different from the normal self-orientated strategy. It has an interconnected nature, and does not recognise separateness. Writing or talking about non-selfishness is likely to be misunderstood or underrated, misinterpretations being possible because the whole cannot be properly grasped by someone in ordinary consciousness.

It has frequently been described as the ineffable – something which is impossible to adequately communicate. Although I am acutely aware of being misunderstood every time I open my mouth or put pen to paper, this risk must be accepted as an occupational hazard if the education of others is to be attempted. (I would refer you back to the comments regarding failure in Chapter 3 as evidence of this difficulty.) People who have studied religion, philosophy, mysticism, and advanced psychology have already acquired a grasp of these concepts. Regrettably, however, the essential perennial truths are invariably mixed up with a lot of unnecessary material. Furthermore, many believe they know something, when in fact they only partly realise what is intended. With this warning in mind, what follows is a concise outline of the formula for a shift to non-selfishness.

There are a few preliminary principles involved:

- ☐ Normal consciousness is not full consciousness.
- ☐ What do you really want: selfishness or non-selfishness?
- ☐ You have the freedom of choice.
- ☐ Knowledge and ability are important, not belief.

The formula for change

These simple principles are practically relevant when approaching the start-line and in applying the formula for change.

Additionally, a few preliminary skills are required:

- ☐ You need to be receptively alert.
- ☐ Concentration will keep you focused.
- ☐ Always be true to yourself.
- ☐ Act now.

These basic skills will assist you to be open and to learn, from both inner and outer experiences, in a consistent way – and then to apply what you know in action. The aim is to deconstruct the limitations of conditioning and to implement a new strategy.

Two main capacities – *seeing* and *feeling* – need to be developed. These abilities are central to the formula and so require careful study. You already possess these capacities. However, they are probably severely under-used, blocked, and distorted. Furthermore, you will have a bias towards one in favour of the other. Both *seeing* and *feeling* must be unfolded and fine tuned. These are unlimited capacities able to bring about a totality of understanding, caring, and empathy. Although natural, they have been buried by avoidance and the culture of selfishness. Like a severely injured person who has to learn how to re-gain the use of his or her arms and legs through numerous physiotherapy sessions – or as with Jonathan Livingston Seagull, in the book of the same name, when he was attempting to go beyond the normally-accepted limitations – it will take much effort and practising for *seeing* and *feeling* to become fully functional. At times of any doubt and despondency, remember your initial choice and decision: selfishness or non-selfishness?

Seeing is a process of enquiry, followed by understanding. It is the tool by which you can expose the conditioned limitations of self-orientated behaviour. *Seeing* begins with a question – not an intellectual question, but one

Actions Speak Louder Than Words

which really has importance to you and must be answered. The question can be simple and general, or it can be specific and personal. "What causes suffering?" "What am I and others doing?" "Am I doing my best?" "How can I do more?" "Why do I feel frustrated?" "Am I limiting my involvement?" "Is this appropriate?" These are just a few examples. The list of questions available for you to ask is endless. By the act of questioning, you are opening up and seeking to go beyond the current boundaries. You are making clear an intention to challenge and investigate, no longer prepared to remain in a semi-closed state of ignoreance. Your questioning needs to be insistent and consistent. Asking a question enables you to search for that "something more" and to examine the possibilities available. The question might be internalised – a personal introspection about yourself – or it may concern someone or something else. Or your enquiry might be a more complex combination of how both interact. Equally, the process of questioning can take the form of a discussion between yourself and others; of course, as indicated above, the motivation needs to be practical and incorporating a sense of urgency.

After asking a question that must be answered, understanding might flood in immediately, dawn gradually, or perhaps only occur after repeated effort and work. Initially, the resulting understanding is likely to be still incomplete in a wider sense and your awareness will almost certainly continue to be contaminated by personal prejudice and elements of avoidance. It is therefore necessary for you to build upon what has been understood through further enquiry. You must keep pushing back the boundaries. Through the repeated asking of appropriate questions, greater comprehension will unfold. This process of expansion might be thought of as picture building. It is similar to the putting together of many fragmented jigsaw pieces to form a coherent picture. One piece (or even several dozen pieces) of a jigsaw puzzle does not reveal the nature of the whole image, although each contains part of the overall content. In its incomplete form, errors of

The formula for change

judgement are possible and to be expected. Beginning to put together the several hundred small pieces of a puzzle, whether you have previously glimpsed the final picture or not, can seem to be a daunting task – especially when you are inexperienced in the techniques of problem solving. A degree of assurance comes with the growing success of linking pieces together, although times of difficulty and frustration may still lie ahead.

The scope of this type of perception and reasoning is much broader than in the case of normal thinking. Recognition of a unifying interconnectedness links together matters which someone less aware might view as unrelated or irrelevant. A wide range of factors might be pertinent to a particular consideration. One thing often leads to another. There is no avoidance or denial. Varying points of view are easy to assess and understand as a cohesive whole. Tendencies which result in divisiveness and exclusion are replaced with an urge to include. Such an alternative way of thinking is open to being misunderstood by those in an ordinary and defensive state of mind.

The effect of *seeing* will, sooner or later, be experienced as an increased awareness. Your perception will become clearer, less hampered by biased misrepresentations and denial. The process of opening up involves a re-cognition of life. You progressively identify first the fact and then the nature and activity of a situation. Certain habitual patterns and mechanisms are realised for what they are – conditioned restrictions. Limiting thoughts, beliefs, emotions, or desires are exposed and you are able to let go. At times, this might be felt as a relief or release. The perceived need for self-defence becomes less and less important to maintain. *Seeing* is a transformational ability which eventually allows a fullness of functioning through total acceptance of reality. It undermines the conditioned "supposed-to-be" games of hide and seek, allowing true freedom and non-selfish individual expression. Selfish desire is superseded by an expanded, inclusive meaning and motivation. Understanding replaces confusion. The interrelatedness of life is intensely appreciated, with personal considerations taking second place.

If *seeing* is the uncluttered ability to reason in a logical and objective manner, *feeling* is the non-rational counterpart which includes the faculty for caring and the sense of belonging. *Feeling* arises from the basic intuition of being part of life. It is a simple but powerful force. It is an unlimited capacity for the love of being, involving a wholeness of concern. *Feeling* is a fullness of relationship. There is non-selfish involvement. It is a compassionate openness which, when experienced, makes denial or turning away impossible. The sense of belonging is unconditional, probably due to it being pre-conditional, and can be considered to be universal. It is an all-inclusive value – pre-moral and pre-cultural – providing a sound and reliable base for more complex ethical considerations.

When *seeing* is neglected or incomplete, there is a degree of irrational, narrow-minded, one-sided thinking. When pure *feeling* is blocked, it is experienced as twisted, unbalanced, and restricted emotion. Together, this results in the various levels and manifestations of dysfunctioning that is ordinary self-orientated consciousness. At one extreme, this behaviour is regarded as sick or pathologically abnormal. At the other end of the range, it is considered as healthy. The mid-range average behaviour is accepted as normal, by popular agreement through numerical domination. Therefore, the absence of complete *seeing* and *feeling* is standard and thus generally unknown. It is a potential, an ideal, or a distant goal.

The way of *seeing* and *feeling* is an interactive process. Greater *seeing* should lead to greater *feeling* – and increased *feeling* should likewise prompt increased *seeing*. If this does not happen, there must be some neglect of the formula. Perhaps the enquiry and understanding is too intellectual or philosophical, avoiding the implications of and for practical reality? Or perhaps there is too much attention on the *feeling* side? Further serious enquiry will reveal where the problem or blockage lies. It is not only a matter of balance, but also of

The formula for change

degree of functioning. Both *seeing* and *feeling* capacities are unlimited.

Seeing and *feeling* are intrinsically related. It is essential that the head and heart are used together, as two integrated parts of a whole. The head without the heart is a cold and sterile place. There is only intellectualisation. The heart adds warmth, a sense of belonging, and meaningfulness. Equally so, the heart alone can be a place of unending sensation – overwhelming, directionless, and indiscriminating – making the beginning of action hard to determine. The head provides the means to rationally assess a situation and consider each part of the whole, allowing preference and priority. *Seeing* and *feeling*, as a combination, provides mature and involved aliveness. These are direct capacities offering a tremendous potential to undo and go beyond all dysfunctional behaviour. They are the faculties of being totally open to life, a means of replacing the present avoidance and "I want more" strategy.

The pace or speed of shifting from selfishness to non-selfishness is determined by the participant. The initial critical factor is that a real beginning should be made. However, as progress occurs and awareness expands, it eventually becomes important to adopt a consistent attitude and approach. The problems of forgetfulness, excuses, and complacency are always waiting to hinder and distract – and this should be remembered. Sincere effort is required for the process to be carried through so that a significant shift can be achieved. This is not a hobby nor an idle interest. There are real consequences involved for all and the change is urgently required.

Once you have gained a significant measure of progress – unlearning most of the old habits, and learning the new formula for a fullness of relationship – the chance of achieving complete transformation becomes possible. But there is a massive problem to resolve. The core difficulty involves the image of separateness. This is the root cause of selfishness. You believe that you are separate. Your strategy has been largely based on the acceptance of this assumption. Bursting the bubble of this central myth is the final hurdle to overcome. After becoming familiar with the theory and practice of the way of *seeing* and *feeling* – in both an inner and outer context (see next chapter) – it then becomes a matter of accelerating and broadening the whole process to all aspects of your life. If everyone does some of this, some of the time (perhaps without necessarily realising so) – an advanced participant in the process will be doing most of it, most of the time; what remains is to do all of it, all of the time. Having initially concentrated on dissolving the secondary mechanisms of avoidance and desire, enquiry will now need to become more intensely focused on the primary image of separateness. *Feeling* must become as pure and open as possible. The way of surrender, which we are about to examine, should be applied without reserve.

The way of *seeing* and *feeling* is an internalised procedure. It must be matched with an outer response, which can be called the way of surrender. Becoming aware of something which demands changing, and sensing a concern that this should happen, leads the aspirant to the point of actually letting go. The old and redundant must be dumped to make way for the new. This requires de-attachment. Sometimes, this letting go might be easy to do. On other occasions, the process of release can be harder to achieve. In the latter instances, additional *seeing* will usually reveal a deeper or secondary attachment/identification; this previously hidden entanglement should also be worked out. Letting go of all selfish restrictions is part of the way of surrender. Sometimes it may simply involve an internal adjustment, but usually an external change is also required. Letting go is a necessary part of the unlearning process.

If there is no compulsive desire, what is left? The non-selfish equivalent is a combination of appropriateness and preferences. Assessing what is appropriate is determined through *seeing* and *feeling*. This all-embracing methodology is infinitely more reliable than the "right" and "wrong" morality of a particular society, in any country or period of

The formula for change

time, which is likely to fluctuate. The needs of both the whole and all the parts are embraced in any evaluation. Assessing appropriateness is the first concern, after which any remaining scope for choice can be settled through preference. Self-orientated considerations obviously have no place in determining appropriateness.

The first stage of evaluation has to assess whether a situation or action is appropriate or inappropriate. A second stage (where required) might decide on the degree of appropriateness between two or more options; various factors could be relevant, such as the perceived priority and/or the degree of overall appropriateness. If a selection of available choices still remains, individual preference should finally be exercised. This alternative system of deciding how to act is based on the mature psychological health characterised by *seeing* and *feeling*. Where someone is still in the process of making the shift, he or she must be conscious of the likelihood of selfish bias, limitations, and avoidance creeping into the above-mentioned practice of assessing appropriateness and preferences – thereby confusing, spoiling, and distorting the outcome. The correct procedure or right tools in immature hands are often useless or even dangerous. Self-orientated people will readily employ an advanced concept to cover up their own inadequacies and make themselves seem intelligent.

Seeing and *feeling* generates a different emphasis – a new importance. The way of surrender then becomes possible, involving a letting go of restrictive self-orientated ways. Compulsive desire is replaced by a system of appropriateness and preferences. This produces a shift from the selfish strategy and exploitative lifestyle towards outer non-selfish action. Appropriate giving and service is the natural consequence of *seeing* and *feeling*. Self-preoccupation fades away in favour of caring for and helping others. Realisation that it is the whole which matters, not just a part in isolation, prompts increased surrender of selfish wants; the needs of the whole are perceived without selfish blinkers. Letting go clears the space, assessment of appropriateness identifies relevant areas of need, non-selfish action through giving and service translates this into outer practice, and the scope for preferences continues the uniqueness of individuality.

This outline of the formula for change is straightforward and direct. There are no mysterious techniques involved. Anything else is non-essential and may well be a distracting waste of time. There is no need for belief or mumbo-jumbo, and little philosophy is required. The formula is therefore potentially acceptable to anyone interested in a better way. The simple nature of the task must be applied throughout the present complexity of your life. You might underestimate the depth and scope of this simplicity. Each foundation of the two alternatives – selfishness and non-selfishness – is fundamentally different; precise understanding of these dissimilar starting points is crucial.....thus the need to begin again by drawing back to the start-line. If the foundation is wrong, no amount of adjustment, growth, or empowering will solve the problem. Most people resist recognising the far-ranging extent of selfishness or self-orientated behaviour, as the stark truth might be painful to accept. Yet avoidance and half-measures result in pseudo-change. Greater seriousness is required. You cannot have things both ways. The choice is clear: selfishness or non-selfishness? Hypocritical mumblings and superficial head-nodding may fool some of the people, some of the time – and probably the person doing it – but such two-faced insincerity makes little or no constructive difference in reality. Until this is honestly acknowledged, the failure of sustained spirituality will continue.

27

The anti-hypocrisy test

The majority of people like to think of themselves as being basically good. And they want to be liked by others. To sustain this image of acceptability and self-esteem, a self-defence system has to be maintained. The usual strategy is to employ one or more forms of avoidance. Life is perceived through filters. You see what you want to see, and hear what you want to hear. Awkward, discomfortable situations and facts are justified, side-stepped, quickly forgotten, or even denied. Hypocrisy is therefore often hard to see in yourself. The multiple pretence of most people makes unconditional honesty an even rarer event. Duplicity and deception become the norm – but are generally not recognised as signs of insincerity, except in blatantly obvious cases. Part of the explanation for this is due to one of the main messages of conditioning: conform; do not rock the proverbial boat. Within this widespread two-facedness are the various philosophical/religious/spiritual groups – well-intentioned people searching for a greater meaning and a better way. But does the insincerity magically vanish just because someone develops an interest in higher matters? Probably not, if we are candid. And so a smug, sanctimonious attitude arises – or perhaps a bland "Oh, how wonderful!" veneer develops. Existing avoidance and self-deception is usually not admitted, and so continues largely unchecked in one form or another. There is not enough openness and plain speaking. In over-looking this important psychological element, the promise of human potential invariably remains limited and thwarted.

We urgently need an anti-hypocrisy test. My suggestion is that actions speak louder than words. This test is not infallible, but it is a generally reliable indicator. In the short-term, an assessment based on outer performance might be misleading; anyone can shine for a day. But over a longer period of time, the true nature of someone's commitment will become obvious. Hidden weaknesses and false claims will sooner or later be exposed. Words come cheap, but consistent action is harder to sustain unless genuinely motivated. Good intentions promise much – and we should take notice of such overtures – yet it is their delivery which provides hard evidence of integrity.

I cannot emphasise the need for this anti-hypocrisy test enough. Its importance is hopefully reflected through being the title of this book. It is time for those with a stated interest in non-selfishness, spirituality, love and understanding, or anything similar to put up or shut up. A token effort to match your words or beliefs is not enough. The grip of selfishness remains. Suffering continues.

Most people's idea of spirituality is some vague notion of detached peacefulness. But this is only half of the picture. There is also an involved aliveness. (This mentality of detached-involvement may seem contradictory. Nevertheless, both qualities are possible as an integrated whole.) What should a Nazi guard in a concentration camp feel? Or someone who sees television pictures of famine in Ethiopia? Who is healthier and more mature: the person troubled with an acute sense of conscience – or another who is able to apparently maintain an easy-going, care-free, "I'm okay" acceptance of the situation? Should an advanced individual not feel some kind of outrage when faced with such appalling circumstances? Is being well-adjusted to society necessarily a good thing if the society has many problems and flaws? Rather than merely "fitting in" and playing the "supposed-to-be" game, isn't it better to struggle for change?

Action must follow awareness, otherwise the awareness is hollow. There has to be a combination between inner and outer transformation. Increased thinking and caring should be matched, step by step, by appropriate action. As the process of *seeing* and *feeling* develops, linked to the way of surrender, it must be accompanied by an equivalent shift in

The anti-hypocrisy test

outer behaviour. If this does not happen, the so-called change is merely internal, incomplete, hypocritical, and thus false. Much of what is regarded as spiritual or personal growth is little more than self-indulgence. The capacity for mutual self-deception is common throughout the various organisations and groups.

As the effect of *seeing* and *feeling* deepens, it is experienced as an opening up to a fullness of reality. There is less avoidance and denial, with distractions having decreased importance, leaving the way more clear for a greater relationship with life. With a broader perception of reality occurring, further enquiry should stimulate you into asking what you are prepared to do in response. The sense of responsibility thereby increases. Action is demanded.

All aspects of your lifestyle have to be reviewed. What is appropriate? And what is not? That which was applicable to the self-orientated mind-set requires re-examining to see if it is in accordance with the non-selfish paradigm. Adjustments will be necessary. If your perceptions, thinking, caring, and values are changing, a corresponding shift in exterior activity should also take place for the transformation to be balanced and properly established. This is where a person's self-honesty and sincerity is put to the test. Will someone conveniently ignore a certain cherished area in the course of his or her questioning? Will the process of letting go be resisted, perhaps through some continued excuse? Will the concept of appropriateness be distorted and abused in the cause of self-interest? What will actually change? What was your decision: selfishness or non-selfishness?

In facing reality, put yourself in someone else's shoes. Go beyond the confines of your own limited preoccupations. What are the results of selfishness? Imagine a child in former Yugoslavia who has had a grenade explode in front of him, now handless and blind in both eyes. What must it be like not having access to even basic health care for families living in a country like Ethiopia or Sudan? How does someone feel who has been raped? And what hurtful experiences turned someone's child into eventually becoming a rapist? Are you sensitive to the primary emotions felt by wildlife when they are butchered by poachers or expelled from an area of natural habitat just to make way for another industrial estate? Do you realise where consumer products come from and what the environmental consequences of the "I want more" mentality are leading towards? In such instances, mere words rightly seem inadequate. A fundamental shift in human activity is the only way these unnecessary episodes will finally be relegated to the history books. We are each a part of the whole – part of the problem, or part of a solution.

By becoming truly involved in a process of change, you are likely to overcome the feelings of powerlessness, frustration, and pessimism which many people who are alert to social injustices experience. The problem itself is undoubtedly a negative issue, but doing something about it is a constructive use of your life. Facing extreme suffering need not be depressing.....if you are willing to interact and work hard for a solution. Enjoyment is normally associated with avoidance of harsh reality, perhaps involving some degree of escapism. However, a deeper form of enjoyment is possible through non-selfish giving and service. Challenging the fundamental cause of suffering – selfishness – is a direct way of working. Beginning the process by changing yourself prepares against hypocrisy.

Please re-read what I have written in Chapter 3 and Chapter 4 about the reasons why I stopped talking about this human potential in 1979. Remember the story in Chapter 5 about how difficult it is to show someone that they are unknowingly yet compulsively seeing double; be open to the possibility of it being relevant to yourself. Consider again the various difficulties which frustrate people's attempts at change; how they combine to produce a hard nut to crack. You will thereby hopefully appreciate the vital need for an anti-hypocrisy test. Although not infallible, my proposal that actions speak louder than

The anti-hypocrisy test

words should provide a generally reliable method of checking, if used as a sincere reflection on progress. Internal change is not enough. A deep-seated reluctance to recognise the extent of one's own selfishness is likely to block any genuine breakthrough. Therefore, hypocrisy must be sought out and challenged. The running away must stop. It is time to put up or shut up – to stand and deliver.

28

The next step forward in human evolution

Fossil-hunting anthropologists have unearthed a growing amount of evidence revealing our past. Although the details are sketchy and interpretations have often had to be revised – with much further work still being necessary – an outline of human prehistory would seem to be emerging. Findings from molecular genetics have provided additional evidence. Our bipedal ancestors have been traced back several million years. Approximately two million years or more ago, we know that *Homo habilis* existed – a human who made and used stone tools. *Homo erectus* lived about one and a half million years ago; this early human was similar in size to us, but with a smaller brain, able to use fire, and skilled at tool-making. Neanderthal Man, *Homo sapiens neanderthalensis*, was a more recent stage in human development. Eventually, about 40,000 years ago, the modern form of *Homo sapiens* appeared.

When Charles Darwin published his now-famous *The Origin of Species* in the middle of the nineteenth century, he hinted about the origin of humans. Many were shocked at the notion of divine creation being questioned – horrified that we might be animals, albeit advanced ones. The Bishop of Worcester's wife is said to have exclaimed: "My dear, descended from the apes! Let us hope it is not true. But if it is, let us pray that it will not become generally known." (In fact, we have not evolved from the chimpanzees and gorillas; rather, at some time in the past, we shared with them a common ancestor.) A number of amusing cartoons reflected the conflict of the time; some depicted apes and other animals as being equally surprised at learning about their human relatives. It is also relevant to note that popular belief accepted as true the Biblical implication that Earth was about

The next step forward in human evolution

6,000 years old. (Modern science estimates our planet is 4,600 million years old, and the Universe much older.) Although the majority of people today acknowledge the evidence and general theory of evolution, many creationists still refuse to do so – which would at least please the Bishop's wife!

Everyone can agree that significant progress has been made in the fields of technology and medical science – even in the past hundred years. We can fly around the world in airplanes, perform complex surgery on the human body, and are beginning the early stages of space exploration. Television sets, computers, and cars are an everyday part of modern life. We may not always concur with all aspects of how this technological advance is currently used, but the knowledge of manipulation has certainly been achieved.

So, if the evidence demonstrates that we have evolved and progressed this far, it is logical to assume that we can develop further. People who negatively shrug their shoulders when the option of radical change is mentioned – they usually blame "human nature" as if it is something fixed or cast in concrete – are in denial of the facts, as well as passing the buck in an attempt to avoid responsibility. If non-selfishness has been achieved by a few pioneering individuals, and glimpsed by many more, it must be possible for this potential to be our future destiny. Just as *Homo habilis* and *Homo erectus* are now our ancestors, surely the present selfishness could also one day become part of the human race's past? Slavery was legal and commonplace just two hundred years ago, involving considerable financial benefits to many influencial people – but, with effort and personal sacrifice, the case for abolition and freedom for all was eventually won. Perhaps a time might come when the human population will see the accepted selfishness of today's culture as inexcusable? If and when this happens is, of course, up to each and every one of us.....starting now.

We are biologically conditioned for self-preservation. If a rhino charges at us – or, to use a more frequently encountered modern example, if a car accidentally threatens to knock us down – we immediately respond.

Actions Speak Louder Than Words

When danger is perceived, the biochemical adrenalin is released and we are able to accelerate into a heightened defensive action. This basic instinctive response to certain situations is obviously an extremely helpful ability. Such beneficial protective strategies would have been a part of the reason for our successful evolution, if the survival of the fittest theory is accepted. These instinctive biological capacities, very different from the cultural psychological conditioning, are compatible with interconnectedness; they provide the means for co-existence in a world of complex species diversity.

As we evolved greater skills, thousands of years ago, settlement and sophisticated culture became possible. Communities sprung up. Person to person interaction became more complicated. Tensions would have escalated, requiring solutions. Human psychology thus developed in response to these intensifying cultural demands, growing out of the primary biological functionings, eventually forming the intricate entanglements that we see today.

We have developed a larger brain size, the ability to make and work with tools, the use of language and a creative urge to express ourselves, and much more. These adaptations have placed us in the position of being the dominant, most advanced species on Earth. We no longer need to struggle against nature for survival. Yet on the negative side, our psychology constantly creates both major and minor problems. It is frequently counter-productive. We fight each other in wars, cheat and steal from our neighbours, and engage in an exploitative "I want more" rat-race. We are sometimes happy, but often discontent. We exist together on the same planet, but pettiness commonly escalates into dysfunctional relationships. To a visiting extraterrestrial, perhaps we might appear to be a bizarre combination of cleverness and stupidity – semi-civilised and semi-barbaric? We have many reasons to be proud of our achievements, but also many reasons to be ashamed if we are honest. We must now face reality without avoidance, and banish complacency until all unnecessary suffering is ended. Then, and only then, will we deserve to call ourselves truly civilised.

Outlining the ruination of a late 1960s community on the west coast of America, *The Last Resort* by The Eagles is a haunting reminder of what we are doing. It is a plea for reconsideration. As everyone knows the frontier stories of how the west was won, they describe their song as telling how the west was lost. Towards the end, the following words are particularly thought-provoking:

> *Who will provide the grand design?*
> *What is yours? And what is mine?*
> *There is no more new frontier*
> *We have got to make it here.*
>
> *We satisfy our endless needs*
> *And justify our bloody deeds*
> *In the name of destiny*
> *In the name of God.*

The song is still as relevant today, continuing to beg our attention, over 20 years after it was written.

Technological progress is advancing rapidly. Access to information has become imperative to those who wish to keep up with this fast pace. Increased opportunities are available. All of which are producing an accelerated way of life, especially in the cities and towns. Can we properly assimilate this mass of data? Can the politicians and other policy makers in society keep up? Are we likely to continue the mad rush ahead without due care and consideration? Will further technological progress help solve our current problems? Or do we need to pause and ask ourselves some fundamental questions? What alternatives exist? Are we choosing the direction forward from a well-informed perspective, or being led sheep-like by those with some vested interest in the kind of future they want to see happen?

The advancement of our psychological health is lagging behind the growth of our technological knowledge. Can we responsibly manage this fast pace of outer change? To do so, we must pay more attention to the inner world behind human activity. There has to be a balanced relationship between the inner and outer experiences. We cannot afford to ignore parts of our mental processes, unless we are willing to accept that the effects of any neglected area may erupt unexpectedly when they can no longer be held back. Knowledge of the world around us needs to be matched with a mature sense of belonging. If people feel isolated and ignored, they will feel resentment and frustration. The old habits of tribalism and group against group divisiveness should be outgrown. The self-orientated approach has to be exposed as the perpetuating cause of our troubles. We all need to recognise our basic humanness and come together.

The enlightenment of humankind, on an individual by individual basis, must be the goal. A complete shift to non-selfishness would be an historical turning point. It would constitute an evolutionary step forward. A change of species identification is warranted by the profound, rudimentary shift in behaviour from selfishness to non-selfishness. This is a fundamental difference, underlying all aspects of being. It marks the end of an old stage – a clear departure from association with an image of separateness – and the start of a new beginning or chapter of human existence. As a pioneer of this evolutionary potential, I suggest that the name *Homo liberalis* might be a suitable candidate for the taxonomic addition. (Whereas *sapiens* means wise, *liberalis* translates as one who is freed, liberated, and generous.)

There are those who are comfortably fitting in with the self-orientated strategy. These people are usually the current "winners", individuals ahead of the main pack. And there are those in the mainstream, neither big-time "winners" nor struggling "losers". This mid-range majority – probably with dreams of being upwardly mobile – are adequately playing the game, although at times with mixed feelings. The "losers" are often those who experience the most discontentment, perhaps as a result of some maladjustment. Many people who do not feel as though they fit in would nevertheless like to if given the chance; their bitterness would disappear if roles were reversed. However, there are some people who genuinely do not want to fit in. They could fit in, and perhaps do so at some level, but they acutely see through the pretence. These are not social misfits, nor the usual type of person who confuses escapism from reality with the search for that "something more". Such individuals have invariably had some experience or insight which has left them feeling like a stranger in a strange land. In certain cases, there has been a significant breakdown of identification with what is "supposed-to-be". The dream on sale no longer tempts. This produces a sincere searching for that "something more". Unfortunately though, a breakthrough is invariably frustrated due to the widespread absence of complete direct knowledge of an alternative. The bubble of selfishness remains unburst. Where are the truly non-selfish examples?

It is outrageous that millions of our fellow human beings continue to die unnecessarily each year of diseases which are easy to cure. It is also shameful that millions of animals are slaughtered annually for human pleasure and enjoyment. And we carry on exploiting the planet's natural resources, despite so-called environmental awareness, threatening the very existence of unique species of wildlife.....and perhaps the entire global well-being of nature. What organisations can we trust to tell the truth and responsibly act on our behalf? Teenagers turn to neighbourhood gangs for love and a sense of belonging. Others turn to heroin, alcohol, or a shopping trip for relief. Somewhere, another 10-year-old girl is raped.

We tolerate too much that needs to be changed. We have created a culture of selfishness and avoidance. We distract ourselves by focusing on the shallow and the cosmetic. We moan and bitch, cleverly avoiding the-buck-stops-here variety of responsibility. We accept and promote mediocrity. We hide behind masks and intelligent-sounding jargon. Until we suffer ourselves. Then we painfully recognise a little of what is wrong.

Actions Speak Louder Than Words

We need to go beyond the superficial responses. We have to ask the awkward questions which few dare to ask. Repeatedly, until things really change. We need to get to the root of our problems. The self-orientated mind-set must be challenged. We should promote excellence, based on the principle of non-selfishness. We must dare to think more. And care more. And to let go. Outer transformation should follow any inner awareness. We must consistently apply the anti-hypocrisy test: *actions speak louder than words.*

Epilgue:
And on.....and on...?

I am writing these final words having just returned from a field trip to Nepal. We built an education centre in a mountain village to encourage nature conservation, to promote better awareness of health care, and to present information about the negative side of what is happening in the so-called developed countries. Shiba and Prem, a young Nepali couple, are leading the project. When we met them a year ago, during our previous visit, their second child was born. Shortly after we left on that occasion, the baby developed a respiratory tract infection and died. Access to £1 worth of medicine – a course of antibiotics – would have probably prevented the unnecessary death. Shiba and Prem decided not to tell us the bad news by letter; thus, we only found out about their tragic loss a few weeks ago. The biggest cause of infant mortality in Nepal is diarrhoea, with between 30,000 and 40,000 deaths occurring each year. Meanwhile, many western tourists travel to Nepal to enjoy a holiday amidst the beautiful Himalayan scenery.....

The aim of this book is to challenge the culture of selfishness and to suggest the non-selfish alternative. It should be obvious by now that I am not an idealist with my head in the clouds; I am a realist. And non-selfishness is a real option. It just needs to be properly understood and conscientiously applied.

Given the strength of today's conditioning, it is unlikely that people will be able to let go of their selfish tendencies all at once. Current thinking is firmly embedded in the self-orientated mind-set, reflected through a wide range of human behaviour. However, it should be easy for any serious person to make a reasonably sincere start. First, you need to make a decision about the fundamental choice: selfishness or non-selfishness? Then you must follow it with some kind of action to mark a beginning of the necessary shifting process; this will involve taking less and giving more. There should also be a willingness to face, rather than avoid, a fullness of reality – however initially awkward or uncomfortable this might be.

I hope that *Actions Speak Louder Than Words* and *Human Potential – the search for that "something more"* will be useful as practical reference books for anyone wishing to study and apply this "new" principle of non-selfishness. They are reliable sources of essential information, based on direct experience. Careful reading and re-reading of these texts should assist greater understanding of what is involved: what needs to be unlearned and what needs to be learned.

Letting go of selfish considerations is commonly perceived in terms of personal loss and hardship, involving an agonising choice. Therefore, the usual response is to keep on avoiding. Complacency and inertia continue. But choosing the non-selfish alternative can be an attractive and satisfying use of your life. It is the means to eventually end suffering and make the world a better place. The sacrifice of selfish tendencies is a necessary part of learning how to give.

If you would like to receive news of future publications, information about our charitable work, and/or details of any forthcoming workshops, please write to us – enclosing a stamped addressed envelope. The Human Potential Trust offers a free-of-charge service to assist people who are interested in non-selfishness. We can provide honest feedback to help deepen an appreciation of what is involved. For those who make the decision to shift towards non-selfishness, there is an opportunity to join in our work. Our postal address is as follows:

The Human Potential Trust
The Oasis
Highbrook Lane
West Hoathly
Sussex RH19 4PL
England